A+ Exam Notes™:
DOS®/Windows®

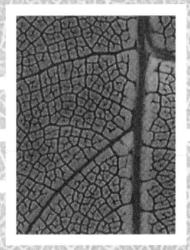

Jim Williams

San Francisco • Paris • Düsseldorf • Soest

Associate Publisher: Guy Hart-Davis
Contracts and Licensing Manager: Kristine Plachy
Acquisitions & Developmental Editor: Neil Edde
Editor: Ronn Jost
Project Editor: Emily Wolman
Technical Editor: Jon Hansen
Book Designer: Bill Gibson
Graphic Illustrator: Tony Jonick
Electronic Publishing Specialist: Bill Gibson
Production Coordinator: Susan Berge
Indexer: Nancy Guenther
Cover Designer: Design Site
Cover Illustrator/Photographer: Design Site

Screen reproductions produced with Collage Complete.

Collage Complete is a trademark of Inner Media Inc.

SYBEX and Exam Notes are registered trademarks of SYBEX Inc.

TRADEMARKS: SYBEX has attempted throughout this book to distinguish proprietary trademarks from descriptive terms by following the capitalization style used by the manufacturer.

The author and publisher have made their best efforts to prepare this book, and the content is based upon final release software whenever possible. Portions of the manuscript may be based upon pre-release versions supplied by software manufacturer(s). The author and the publisher make no representation or warranties of any kind with regard to the completeness or accuracy of the contents herein and accept no liability of any kind including but not limited to performance, merchantability, fitness for any particular purpose, or any losses or damages of any kind caused or alleged to be caused directly or indirectly from this book.

Library of Congress Card Number: 98-86618
ISBN: 0-7821-2346-5

Manufactured in the United States of America

10 9 8 7 6 5 4 3 2 1

I would like to dedicate this book to my kids, Thom, Doug, and Mindy, whose achievements never cease to amaze me; and to my brother, Wm. C. VanHorn, whose stoic wisdom will always be a part of me. Thanks for the inspiration. I love you all.

Acknowledgments

I have always wanted to be an author and now I know what it is like to bring a child of your mind into reality. The long hours, the sweat, and the frustrations are insignificant compared to the immense feelings of accomplishment and satisfaction gained from this experience. I owe this new experience to many different sources.

First and foremost on my list is my Heavenly Father who in his infinite love gave me the ability to write and provided me with the opportunity to author this book.

Then there is the outstanding group of professionals at Sybex who led me through the technical labyrinth of writing for publication. I would like to thank Neil Edde who took the risk of offering me the opportunity for writing this book and then worked with me in developing the correct layout and style for it. I would also like to offer my sincere appreciation to Emily Wolman who kept me on track, offered me untiring support and encouragement, and was so understanding when things started to go awry.

My deepest gratitude goes to Ronn Jost, the chief editor. To Ronn I give the credit for turning my ramblings into a coherent, informative text and for greatly improving my abilities as a writer. I would also like to thank Jon Hansen for the work he did in ensuring the technical subject matter was as precise as possible. Until writing this book, I never realized how many different viewpoints existed for some of the finer points of operating systems.

Then there is the production crew, who took the text and screen captures and turned them into their final form. My thanks and admiration go to production coordinator Susan Berge, electronic publishing specialist Bill Gibson, and indexer Nancy Guenther for turning my child into the wonderful adult that it is.

They say that behind every great endeavor there stands a woman. I have two to whom I owe my life. Love and thanks to my wife, Melinda, who put up with my crazy hours and early morning ranting, and even force fed me a couple of times. Love and thanks also to my mother, Anne, who quietly accepted my prolonged absences and missed visits.

Finally, I would like to thank the readers of this book. You are the basis of what makes our country strong. Your ambitions to improve your skills and your way of life by becoming a certified professional are in the same character as our Founding Fathers. May God bless you in your efforts.

Table of Contents

Introduction

If you've purchased this book, you must be in pursuit of your A+ certification. This is a great goal, and it is also a great career builder. If you glance through any newspaper, you'll find employment opportunities for A+ certified computer professionals—these ads are there because finding qualified employees is a challenge in today's market. The certification means you know something about how computers and computer operating systems work, but more importantly, it means you have the ability, determination, and focus to learn—the greatest skills any employee can have!

What Is A+ Certification?

A+ is a certification program designed to quantify the level of critical thinking skills and general industry knowledge demanded of computer service technicians. It was developed by the Computer Technology Industry Association (CompTIA) to provide an industry-wide recognition of those service technicians who have attained this level of knowledge. For example, Novell has developed their Certified Novell Engineer (CNE) program to provide the same recognition for network professionals that deal with their NetWare products. Also, Microsoft has their Microsoft Certified Service Engineer (MCSE) program. The theory behind these certifications is that if you need to have service performed on any of their products, a technician who has been certified in one of their certification programs should be the one you call, since they know the product.

The A+ certification program was created to be a wide-ranging certification involving products from many vendors. In any case, if any computer service is needed, an A+ certified technician should be able to solve the problem.

What Is an AASC?

More service companies are becoming A+ Authorized Service Centers (AASCs). This means that over 50 percent of the technicians employed by that service center are A+ certified. At the time of the writing of this book, there are over 1,400 A+ Authorized Service Centers in the world. Customers and vendors are recognizing that AASCs employ the most qualified service technicians. Because of this, an AASC will get more business than a nonauthorized service center. Because more service centers want to reach the AASC level, they will give preference to a candidate who is A+ certified rather than one who is not. Also, they have an idea of the level of knowledge of the job candidate.

Is This Book for You?

The A+ Exam Notes books were designed to be succinct, portable exam review guides that can be used either in conjunction with a more complete study program (book, CBT courseware, classroom/lab environment) or as an exam review for those who don't feel the need for more extensive test preparation. It isn't our goal to "give the answers away," but rather to identify those topics on which you can expect to be tested and to provide sufficient coverage of these topics.

Perhaps you've been working with computer technologies for years now. The thought of paying lots of money for a specialized A+ exam preparation course probably doesn't sound too appealing. What can they teach you that you don't already know, right? Be careful, though. Many experienced computer professionals have walked confidently into exam centers only to walk sheepishly out of them after failing an A+ exam. As they discovered, there are many computer-related technologies that people take for granted in the everyday world; when presented with detailed exam questions on these topics, their everyday knowledge can fail them. After you've finished reading through this book, you should have a clear idea of how your understanding of the technologies involved matches up with the expectations of the A+ exam makers at CompTIA.

Or perhaps you're relatively new to the world of computers, drawn to it by the promise of challenging work and higher salaries. You've just waded through an 800-page A+ study guide or taken a class at a local training center. Lots of information to keep track of, isn't it? Well, by organizing the Exam Notes books according to the official CompTIA A+ exam objectives, and by breaking up the information into concise, manageable pieces, we've created what we think is the handiest exam review guide available. Throw it in your briefcase and carry it to work with you. As you read through the book, you'll be able to identify quickly those areas you know best and those that require more in-depth review.

NOTE   The goal of the Exam Notes series is to help A+ candidates familiarize themselves with the subjects on which they can expect to be tested in the exams. For complete, in-depth coverage of the technologies and topics involved, we recommend the *A+: DOS/Windows Study Guide, Second Edition*, Sybex, 1998.

How Is This Book Organized?

As mentioned above, this book is organized according to the official exam objectives list prepared by CompTIA for the A+: DOS/Windows exam. The chapters coincide with the broad objectives groupings, such as Function, Structure, Operation, and File Management, and Memory Management.

Within each chapter, the individual exam objectives are addressed in turn. And in turn, the objectives sections are further divided according to the type of information presented.

Critical Information

This section presents the greatest level of detail on information that is relevant to the objective. This is the place to start if you're unfamiliar with or uncertain about the technical issues related to the objective.

Necessary Procedures

Here you'll find instructions for procedures that require a lab computer to be completed. From installing operating systems to modifying configuration defaults, the information in these sections addresses the hands-on requirements for the A+ exams.

NOTE Not every objective has procedures associated with it. For such objectives, the "Necessary Procedures" section has been left out.

Exam Essentials

In this section, we've put together a concise list of the most crucial topics of subject areas that you'll need to comprehend fully prior to taking the A+ exam. This section can help you identify those topics that might require more study on your part.

Key Terms and Concepts

Here we've compiled a mini-glossary of the most important terms and concepts related to the specific objective. You'll understand what all those technical words mean within the context of the related subject matter.

Sample Questions

For each objective, we've included a selection of questions similar to those you'll encounter on the actual A+ exam. Answers and explanations are provided so that you can gain some insight into the exam-taking process.

How to Get A+ Certified

A+ certification is available to anyone. You don't have to work for any particular company. It's not a secret society. It is, however, an elite group. To become A+ certified, you must do two things:

- Pass the A+ Certification Core exam

- Pass the A+ Certification Operating System Specialty exam (DOS/ Windows)

These exams are administered by Sylvan Prometric and can be taken at any Sylvan Prometric Testing Center. Once you pass these exams, you will get a certificate in the mail from CompTIA saying that you have passed. To find the Sylvan Prometric testing center nearest you, call (800) 755-EXAM (755-3926).

NOTE   Sybex also publishes the A+: *Core Module Study Guide, Second Edition,* and *A+ Exam Notes: Core Module.* Both are available at bookstores worldwide.

To register for the exams, call Sylvan at (800) 77-MICRO (776-4276). To register, you must give them your name, social security number, mailing address, phone number, employer (if applicable), when and where you want to take the exam (the Sylvan center at which you want to take the exam), and your credit card number to pay the exam fee.

NOTE   For more information on the A+ program, visit the CompTIA Web site at **www.comptia.org**.

Tips for Taking the A+ Exams

Here are some general tips to keep in mind when you go to take your exam:

- Arrive early at the exam center so that you can relax and review your study materials, particularly tables and lists of exam-related information.

- Read the questions carefully. Don't be tempted to jump to an early conclusion. Make sure you know *exactly* what the question is asking.

- Don't leave any unanswered questions. Unanswered questions are scored against you.

- When answering multiple-choice questions you're not sure about, use a process of elimination to get rid of the obviously incorrect answers first. This will improve your odds if you need to make an educated guess.

- Because the hard questions will eat up the most time, save them for last. You can move forward and backward through the exam.

How to Contact the Author

I was well into adulthood before I realized that textbooks are not always correct. I have also found that a task of this nature is full of seemingly contradictory information. In trying to make sense of the different ideas found in my research, I have probably erred in my assumptions or in the way I expressed something.

If you find any errors or wish to contact me for any reason, please feel free to do so. I am a teacher by spirit and an avid learner by nature, so I welcome any constructive advice, critiques, or comments that will improve or correct my knowledge base. My e-mail address is jwilliam@webaccess.net.

How to Contact the Publisher

Sybex welcomes reader feedback on all of their titles. Visit the Sybex Web site at www.sybex.com for book updates and additional certification information. You'll also find online forms to submit comments or suggestions regarding this or any other Sybex book.

CHAPTER

1

Function, Structure, Operation, and File Management

A+ Exam Objectives Covered in This Chapter:

▶ **Identify the operating system's functions, structure, and major system files.** *(pages 3 – 28)*

▶ **Identify ways to navigate the operating system and how to get to needed technical information.** *(pages 28 – 40)*

▶ **Identify basic concepts and procedures for creating, viewing, and managing files and directories, including procedures for changing file attributes and the ramifications of changes (for example, security issues).** *(pages 40 – 51)*

▶ **Identify the procedures for basic disk management.** *(pages 52 – 63)*

T he objectives of this domain require knowledge of the DOS, Windows 3.*x*, and Windows 95 operating systems, including their functions and structures, managing files and directories, and running programs. It also includes navigating through the operating system from DOS command-line prompts and the Windows procedures for accessing and retrieving information.

The major purpose of this domain is to test your knowledge of the major concepts, functions, structures, commands, and utilities associated with DOS, Windows 3.*x*, and Windows 95 operating-system environments. A thorough understanding of this material will help you troubleshoot and diagnose system problems, and increase your skills in recognizing and resolving problems associated with a computer's operating system.

NOTE This material is a major portion of the exam (30 percent), so make every effort possible to master the objectives in this section.

Identify the operating system's functions, structure, and major system files.

This objective concentrates primarily on the components and features of the operating system, and the ways it performs its job. You will have to know what the operating system does, how it performs its major tasks, and where the major files, commands, and utilities are located.

Critical Information

Even though most systems being sold today contain Windows 95 (soon to be Windows 98 or Windows NT), a vast number of systems still run the DOS/Windows 3.x operating system. There is a good chance you will still see some plain DOS-based machines due to the requirements of some special-purpose applications (professional accounting packages and industrial control applications are two examples).

With this in mind and because you know that DOS, Windows 3.x, and Windows 95 will be covered on the exam, you will need a well-grounded knowledge of what they do and how they perform their functions. The operating system is the basic element that gives the PC its "intelligence" and turns a useless electronic gadget into a highly productive tool. All PC-based operating systems perform the following functions:

System resource management: Resources include user memory (RAM), hard disk space, interrupts (IRQs), and memory channels (DMAs).

File manipulation: The operating system must allow users to create, delete, move, modify, copy, etc. the files stored on the system's hard disk drive(s).

Input/output (I/O) control: The operating system must also be able to control the data flow into and out of the computer. This includes the keyboard, mouse, serial ports, parallel ports, video, modem, etc. All peripheral devices must pass through one of the computer's access points (I/O ports). Since I/O ports are a scarce resource, the operating system must coordinate the various functions that take place through the I/O ports with the other system requirements.

Program execution: The operating system must be able to run various types of application programs (spreadsheets, word processors, utilities, etc.). To do this, it must be able to accept the machine instructions provided by the program, process them through the CPU, and control the flow of the program as it runs.

Functions of DOS, Windows 3.x, and Windows 95

All operating systems perform the same basic functions. They handle I/O operations, disk management services, memory management, and application interface and control. In this section, DOS will be used to present the major functions common to all operating systems. Windows 3.x can be thought of as a user-friendly add-on to DOS, and Windows 95 can be considered a blending of the DOS operating system and the Windows 3.x user interface.

DOS

DOS is an operating system designed for 16-bit, IBM-compatible microcomputers. It is a basic, command-line–oriented operating system and consists of two major elements—the user interface and the hardware controller. DOS presents itself to the user in the form of a command-line interface that displays a system prompt.

A user must enter command strings at the system prompt (e.g., C:\>), which DOS interprets through the ROM BIOS. Command strings are entered as text strings and follow a syntax to work. Menu utilities such as DOSSHELL are commonly used to make the interface more user friendly.

After the command has been interpreted, DOS controls the execution of the command through the CPU and by manipulating the hardware

(RAM, I/O ports, etc.) needed to successfully complete execution. The functions of DOS include:

Command processing: During the system boot-up process, the DOS command processor is loaded into RAM and the command prompt is displayed. The command prompt indicates that the system has finished the boot-up process and is waiting for you to enter a command. Once a command is entered, the command processor interprets the command and any parameters that are on the command line, and then activates and controls the necessary hardware components to execute the command.

Application services: These services are provided by DOS to the applications that are running, and are usually transparent to the user. When a problem arises from a service request, DOS will notify the user of the problem with a cryptic error message. Some of the services provided by DOS to applications include:

- **Input/output control:** These services provide the application with the ability to use the system's hardware, such as the keyboard and mouse, for input, and the monitor and printer for output.

- **File and directory management:** These services relieve the application of the tasks associated with file management. In DOS, every entry on a storage media is considered to be a file whether it is a document, an application, or a utility. Whenever a file is used, DOS keeps track of where it is located on the storage device and where it places it in RAM. It also tracks any changes made to the file. In addition, DOS keeps track of the directory structure on the storage media by recording the filename, storage location, size of the file, and date and time the file was last changed. Because of these services, the application needs to know only the name of the file and the directory in which the file is located.

- **Memory management:** DOS also manages all associated memory requirements for the application, including the program code itself and its data elements.

System services: DOS controls the movement of program instructions and data into and out of the central processor unit, tracks time for time-sensitive devices, and provides system control and error-reporting capabilities for all system requirements.

DOS commands: In addition to the above services, DOS provides the user with a set of commands that can be used directly from the command line. These commands can be internal (loaded into memory with the operating system) or external (located on a storage device). There are 11 basic categories of DOS commands:

- **Backup:** These commands are used to provide a means of protecting your system in case of a catastrophic failure of your hard disk. These commands include BACKUP.EXE, which compresses and copies the disk files and directory structures to a backup medium such as a tape drive or floppy disks, and RESTORE.EXE, which expands the backup files and replaces them onto the hard disk.

NOTE Prior to DOS 6, the BACKUP and RESTORE commands were tedious and unreliable. With DOS 6, the BACKUP and RESTORE commands were replaced by a much more reliable and easier-to-use version called Microsoft Backup (MSBACKUP.EXE), which is a scaled-down version of Norton Backup.

- **Date/time:** The DATE and TIME commands provide you with the ability to display and set the system time.

- **Diagnostics:** The MSD, CHKDSK, and SCANDISK commands provide a means to check the system parameters, assist in diagnosing system problems, and, in the case of CHKDSK and SCANDISK, fix minor problems with the system.

- **Directory management:** The MD, RD, CD, DELTREE, and MOVE commands allow you to manage the directory tree.

- **Disk management:** MIRROR, DBLSPACE, DRVSPACE, and FASTOPEN are used to protect the file allocation table (FAT), increase storage capacity, and increase disk access speed.

- **Error checking and recovery:** CHKDSK, SCANDISK, and DEFRAG allow you to check for potential system problems and fix many of them.

- **File management:** ATTRIB, COMP, DEL, REN, UNDELETE, MOVE, COPY, and XCOPY provide a means of handling files in an efficient manner.

- **Information display:** DIR, VER, ECHO, HELP, MORE, TYPE, and VOL are helpful in displaying information to the screen.

- **Memory management:** MEM, MEMMAKER, DEVICEHIGH, and LOADHIGH are used to manage memory resources.

- **Menu:** DOSSHELL is a menu utility that allows you to arrange your programs in an environment that is more user friendly.

- **Preparation:** FDISK is used to partition hard disk drives, and FORMAT is used to ready both floppy and hard disk drives for data storage. SYS is used to transfer the system files onto a floppy or hard disk drive.

Windows 3.x

Windows 3.x is a directory-oriented graphical user interface (GUI) that works in conjunction with DOS to provide a more user-friendly, multi-tasking environment. In and of itself, Windows 3.x is not an operating system—it is a shell, an extra layer of interface between the user and DOS, that adds additional capabilities and makes the operating system easier to use.

Windows 3.x relies on the DOS operating system for most of its functionality. Since it is a GUI, the user interface consists of a series of screen displays or windows that contain icons (small pictures that represent the programs they launch), menu bars, and feature bars. Added functions include:

Multi-tasking capability: Windows 3.x is considered to be a *cooperative multi-tasking* environment. This means that the Windows environment can effectively run more than one application at a time. Since each application is responsible for its use and release of system resources, the applications work within a cooperative multi-tasking environment.

Cut and paste: Windows 3.*x* can copy or cut material from one application and paste it into another application through the use of the Clipboard, which is a memory buffer that keeps the image or text that was copied or cut into it.

Common user interface (CUI): Windows 3.*x*'s CUI feature gives all Windows-based applications the same look and feel as the Windows interface. This makes working with Windows applications much easier. Common elements include the mouse pointer and its click, double-click, and click-and-drag operations; the common theme for the design of the windows; and the manner in which menu bars display drop-down menus, dialog boxes, and other user-interface tools.

Interprocess communications or Object Linking and Embedding (OLE): This feature allows a user to design documents that can actually use data from other documents.

- *Linking* is when you create an active link between a host document and a client document. When you change data in the host, it will automatically change the data in the client document.

- *Embedding* is when a graphic, text, or file from one application is embedded into another document. The embedded data are not automatically updated when the original document is changed, but they are still connected to the application that was used to create it.

NOTE Windows 3.11 can also connect a peer-to-peer network that allows users to share files, printers, CD-ROM drives, and other resources. See Chapter 5 for the details.

Windows 95

Windows 95 is an operating system designed for 32-bit, IBM-compatible microcomputer architectures. It is a *document-oriented, GUI-based* operating system. In it, Microsoft has combined the components of DOS with the elements of a GUI and added some additional features such as *preemptive multi-tasking* and plug-and-play hardware detection to produce their new type of operating system, which has the look and feel of the Apple Macintosh operating system. Windows 95 has gained widespread popularity and continues to replace earlier legacy operating systems.

Windows 95 performs all the functions listed in the sections on DOS and Windows 3.*x*, and has the following additional functions:

Support for the Plug-and-Play (PnP) standard: The PnP standard allows Windows 95 to detect the types of hardware attached to the computer system. It queries all attached devices and, if they are PnP compatible, it determines what they are and what parameters it needs to set for them.

Preemptive multi-tasking environment: This type of operating system controls the system resources and allocates an amount of time for each application to use. It then cycles through the active applications, polling them for resource requirements, and allocates the needed resources to each in turn, depending on need and priority. If one application hangs, the operating system removes the system resources from it when the application's allotted time runs out; if it is still hung on the next poll, the operating system passes it by. This way, the system *should* never lock up.

Major Components of DOS, Windows 3.*x*, and Windows 95

The major components of an operating system are the elements that make the system work, give it its look and feel, and allow users to control the hardware and applications.

DOS

The major components of DOS are the boot files, COMMAND.COM, environment variables, and external commands.

- The *boot files* are two hidden files, IO.SYS and MSDOS.SYS, that perform the boot-up process.

- COMMAND.COM is the command interpreter and user interface. It also contains the *internal commands* (DIR, TYPE, COPY, etc.), which are loaded into memory with the operating system during the boot-up process. COMMAND.COM is located in the root directory of the primary hard disk drive.

- *Environment variables* or *parameters* are system elements used to modify the way the system works, and are used extensively in batch files. There are two types of parameters: DOS parameters and command-line execution parameters. DOS parameters (SET PROMPT, DATE, etc.) are global in nature and are used within a batch file much like programming variables are used in computer programs. The command-line execution parameters are used on the command line following the batch filename to pass variable information into the batch file for processing.

- The *external commands* (XCOPY, FDISK, FORMAT, CHKDSK, etc.) are the utilities supplied with DOS and are located in the DOS directory on the hard disk drive.

When DOS has completed loading, the system displays a *command prompt* that indicates the system is ready to use. Here, users type in their command strings to make DOS do their bidding.

Windows 3.x

Since Windows 3.x is only a GUI to DOS, it has the same components as DOS. The additional components that make up Windows 3.x are as follows:

Desktop: Windows 3.x's screen display is called the *desktop*. All actions are initiated at the desktop, which displays executable programs and utilities as icons.

Menu bars: Major options are listed on the *menu bar* located across the top of the screen. Additional menus called drop-down menus may be used to show options in submenus.

Miscellaneous boxes: Different types of boxes are used within Windows 3.x to communicate with the user.

- **Dialog boxes:** *Dialog boxes* are used to gain additional information from the user. Windows will display a message prompting the user for the information, and the user types in the information.

- **List boxes:** *List boxes* are also used to obtain additional information from the user. Windows displays a box with a list of items; the user selects the item or items needed.

- **Feature boxes:** Feature boxes display a list of options from which the user selects the single item needed.

Windows displays its screens in the form of windows—rectangular areas on the screen. There are two types of windows—*application windows*, which display the features of an application (such as a word processor, spreadsheet, or database program) you have activated, and *document windows*, which display the contents of a file on which you are working. Multiple windows can be displayed on the screen in any combination and arranged on the desktop much like you would do on a real desk.

Windows 95

Windows 95 contains many of the same components as DOS/Windows 3.*x*, including system files, various types of windows, icons, menu bars, the desktop, and the different types of interactive boxes.

Desktop: The screen display is called the *desktop*, but it is a completely restructured display that more readily resembles a real desktop. It provides a location to place *folders* (containers that hold files or other folders [*subfolders*]), *files* (documents), and *programs* (applications or utilities). They can be placed anywhere on the desktop—just like with a real desk.

Taskbar: The *Taskbar* shows the list of active programs and open folders. The programs are represented by small, labeled areas on the Taskbar.

Start menu button: The Start menu button activates a pop-up menu listing the programs you have assigned to the StartUp folder. You can launch new programs by clicking either an application file or a document file, which will launch the program that is associated with it and then load the document into the application window.

Contrasts between Windows 3.*x* and Windows 95

Windows 3.*x* and Windows 95 share many of the same basic features. The major areas of contrast are listed below.

Multi-tasking operating system: Windows 3.*x* uses a *cooperative multi-tasking environment,* while Windows 95 uses a more reliable and consistent *preemptive multi-tasking environment.* This reduces the amount of general protection faults (GPFs) and system lockups.

Document-centric vs. application-centric: Windows 95 is *document-centric* rather than *application-centric* like Windows 3.*x* and DOS. The central focus of your work is on the documents you create instead of the application that created them. This makes the desktop a more realistic workplace. Folders (document and tool containers) are placed on your desktop. You can activate an application through the document and load the document at the same time. You can also launch an application and then retrieve any document you wish.

Hierarchy tree: In Windows 3.*x*, the file structure is based around a directory that features the *root directory* as the top-level directory with subdirectories and files under it. The hierarchy in Windows 95 is organized with the desktop at the top of the tree. My Computer and Network Neighborhood make up the second level, and the third level contains the disk drives with their root directories, folders, subfolders, and files.

32-bit vs. 16-bit operation: Windows 3.*x* utilizes only 16 bits for its operations, data transfer, and control handlers. Most of the facilities within Windows 95 use 32 bits, which provides for faster data transfer and more control codes for data protection.

Plug and Play (PnP): Windows uses a device identification standard that allows PnP-compatible devices to correctly identify themselves to the operating system. This feature automates the installation process and shaves hours off the setup time for configuring new devices added to the system.

Memory management: Windows 95 can trick DOS-based programs into thinking that they each have the 640KB RAM conventional memory to themselves. This allows most DOS programs to run much more efficiently within the Windows 95 environment. Windows is also capable of using virtual memory to help tame some of the more memory-hungry applications and keep them from crashing the system.

Long filenames: Windows 95 is not limited to the 8.3 file-naming convention associated with DOS and Windows 3.*x*. You can use up to 255 characters for a filename. For legacy programs, Windows 95 keeps an 8.3 record name for each long filename as well.

Explorer: Windows 95 has a new and vastly improved file-management system called Explorer. The Explorer window is divided into two panes. The left pane displays the entire contents of the desktop hierarchy, including the folders in your directory structure; the right pane shows the files and/or folders of the selected item.

Super mouse: Windows 95 assigns operations to both mouse buttons. The right (or secondary) mouse button is now used. If you right-click the mouse, you receive a list of options that include creating or renaming a folder, deleting files, and getting information about the file, folder, or device properties.

Shortcuts: Windows 95 allows you to create icons called *shortcuts* that point to a user-specified program or document. Shortcuts can be placed anywhere within the system—on the desktop or in any folder on any accessible drive.

Major System Files

System files are the files that contain the operating system's programming code, configuration definition, system commands, or system utilities. The following files are the essential system files for DOS, Windows 3.*x*, and Windows 95.

DOS

IO.SYS, MSDOS.SYS, CONFIG.SYS, COMMAND.COM, and AUTOEXEC.BAT are the major system files found in DOS. They are used to activate and configure the operating system during the boot-up process. These major system files are located in the root directory of the primary hard disk drive (usually C:) and must be executed in the following order:

IO.SYS: A binary file that provides the basic input/output interface between the ROM BIOS and the hardware.

MSDOS.SYS: A binary file considered to be the core of the DOS operating system containing the disk-manipulation routines.

CONFIG.SYS: A text file used to load drivers (RAM disk, display, keyboard, etc.) and Terminate and Stay Resident (TSR) programs (memory managers, virus checkers, etc.) that configure the system to the user's needs. It is also used to set the sizes for the FILES, BUFFERS, and STACKS parameters.

COMMAND.COM: This file is the user interface and contains the internal DOS commands. It is also the part of the operating system that displays the DOS prompt and interprets the commands entered on the command line.

AUTOEXEC.BAT: An optional text file that contains DOS commands that the user wants to run automatically each time the systems boots. It is also used to set the search paths, prompt display, and other system variables.

These files are loaded in a sequential order following the completion of the power on self test (POST). The CONFIG.SYS and AUTOEXEC .BAT files are optional and are not needed for booting DOS. Without AUTOEXEC.BAT present, the system will display the DATE and TIME commands.

TIP A system backup disk should be created to help recover from a system crash. You should include the AUTOEXEC.BAT and CONFIG.SYS files on a bootable diskette along with any special drivers for the CD-ROM, video, etc.

Windows 3.x

The major system files used with Windows 3.x are PROGMAN.EXE, WIN.COM, USER.EXE, GDI.EXE, KRNLxxx.EXE, WIN.INI, SYSTEM.INI, and WIN386.EXE.

PROGMAN.EXE: This file is the Program Manager—it executes and manages the programs with which you are working. It is the first screen that you see after Windows finishes booting.

WIN.COM: This is the Windows start-up program that tests the system variables and prepares the environment for Windows. It also displays the Windows logo screen.

USER.EXE: This file is a core system file, and is the user-interface module that accepts input from the user (mouse or keyboard) and passes the data to the appropriate component of Windows.

GDI.EXE: This is another core system file, and is the file for the graphical device interface manager. Its major purpose is to manage graphics and printing. It is the interface between Windows and graphics and the printer, whichever is designated as the output at the time.

KRNL*xxx*.EXE: This file is also a core system file and makes up the backbone of Windows. It manages the Windows resources and the running applications. KERNL386.EXE is used when Windows is in Enhanced mode; KERNL286.EXE is used when Windows is in Standard mode. These files perform the same functions as IO.SYS— they handle base functions such as memory management, file I/O, and application loading and executions.

WIN.INI: This is a system-initialization file (and a text file) whose purpose is to contain the Windows environmental settings that control the general function and appearance of the Windows display.

SYSTEM.INI: This is the system-initialization file that contains the Windows configuration settings concerning the hardware setup, active drivers, and system settings for the Windows environment.

WIN386.EXE: Handles all virtual memory devices, manages virtual machines, and converts extended memory to expanded memory for MS-DOS–based applications.

Windows 95

The major system files used with Windows 95 are IO.SYS, MSDOS.SYS, COMMAND.COM, WIN.INI, PROGMAN.INI, SYSTEM.DAT, and USER.DAT.

IO.SYS: This file performs the same basic functions as the Windows 3.*x* file. It has been enhanced to meet the needs of Plug-and-Play technology.

MSDOS.SYS: As in Windows 3.*x*, this file is also the main file for the operating system. It performs the same functions as the Windows 3.*x* file, but is greatly enhanced to handle the preemptive multi-tasking capabilities of Windows 95.

COMMAND.COM: This file, like its counterpart in Windows 3.*x*, is the user interface and command interpreter. It includes many of the features once contained in the Windows 3.*x* CONFIG.SYS file.

WIN.INI: This file and SYSTEM.INI have been replaced by the Windows 95 Registry database. They are used only for backward compatibility with Windows 3.*x* applications.

PROGMAN.INI: This file is the same as the Windows 3.*x* version.

SYSTEM.DAT: This file contains the machine-specific information needed by the Registry. This file is located in the C:\WINDOWS directory.

USER.DAT: This file contains the user-specific information the system needs for the Registry, and is located in the C:\WINDOWS directory on stand-alone machines and in the user's home directory for networked PCs.

System, Configuration, and User-Interface Files

The major system files were covered in the previous section. This section will cover the additional files the system uses for its configuration and the way it interfaces with the user.

DOS

DOS interfaces with the user from a simple command-line prompt as illustrated below. Users must know which commands to use and the proper syntax of the commands before they can get the computer to work for them.

Command lines consist of the DOS prompt (C:\) and the command (dir) as follows:

```
C:\> DIR
```

The following commands are used by DOS, add new features to DOS, set up hardware, change file characteristics, and protect files.

ATTRIB: This command sets the file attributes to Read Only (R), Archive (A), System (S), and Hidden (H). A plus (+) in front of the letter will turn on the attribute, and a minus (–) will turn it off. A Read Only file cannot be deleted or modified until the attribute is turned off. An Archive file indicates whether the file has been changed since the last backup. A System file is set apart for special use by the operating system. A Hidden file is left out of any normal directory displays.

COMMAND.COM: This is the user interface for DOS. It is automatically loaded during the boot-up process. Additional activation of COMMAND.COM invokes another DOS environment shell.

DOSSHELL: This command invokes a menu system for DOS that is fairly easy to set up and use. It can be set up to display your commonly used applications and the directory structure.

EXPAND: This command is used to decompress program files that come on the distribution diskette.

MIRROR: This command protects the hard disk drive from corrupted partition tables and file allocation table errors by keeping a running copy of the FAT and storing a copy of the partition table on a diskette. It can also be used to help restore deleted files.

MODE: The MODE command is used to set parameters for the parallel and serial ports, keyboard, and display adapters.

MSCDEX: This file is an MS-DOS extended command set used to support CD-ROM drives.

SET: The SET command is used to set the values of environmental variables.

In addition to the system commands, you should also be familiar with the following DOS system files:

ANSI.SYS: The text-formatting device driver for screen display

HIMEM.SYS: The *extended* memory manager provided by DOS

EMM386.EXE: The *expanded* memory manager provided by DOS

Windows 3.*x*

The system, configuration, and user-interface files used by Windows 3.*x* include:

PROGMAN.EXE: This is the program file that creates and manages the desktop environment. It is the central part of the Windows interface and allows you to organize your work into groups, launch programs from icons, and work in a multi-tasking environment.

Registry: The configuration information for OLE is stored in this system file. It is a binary database file called REG.DAT located in the SYSTEM subdirectory under the WINDOWS directory. It can be accessed only with a program called REGEDIT.EXE.

WARNING   Messing with the Registry is a highly risky business! Most repairs can be done through other means. If this file gets scrambled, you will have to reload Windows.

DLL files: These are dynamic link library files that are common program segments used by several different Windows programs as needed.

NOTE   If you add games, shareware, and low-cost applications, it can cause trouble with your DLL files. If you experience strange problems after one of these types of programs has been installed, you may want to save time and reinstall Windows after backing up your critical files.

CONTROL.INI: This is a system-initialization file used by the Control Panel and contains the values for the settings most often changed, such as the color scheme and pattern.

PROGMAN.INI: PROGMAN.EXE uses this file to initialize itself as the system loads. It contains two sections—the [Settings] section specifies where and how the Program Manager screen appears on the desktop, and the [Groups] section lists the Group Icon names and their order of access.

WIN.INI: This initialization file is used to store data about the Windows environment such as its color scheme.

SYSTEM.INI: This initialization file contains the information needed by Windows to deal with the hardware connected to the system.

NOTE   When preparing backup disks for restoring your system in the event of a crash, make sure that, at a very minimum, the WIN.INI, SYSTEM.INI, PROGMAN.INI, and *.GRP files are backed up along with the AUTOEXEC.BAT and CONFIG.SYS files. If you have the time and space, you should try to copy all of the *.INI files as well. If you have to reinstall your entire hard disk, these files will return your system to the same look you had before the crash.

Windows uses three basic methods to store its program configuration information. These are the INI files, the Windows Registry, and the group files. The INI files are ASCII text files that contain program-initialization settings. The Registry is a database called REG.DAT that stores environmental settings for various Windows programs and contains information on which applications are associated with which type of file extension. The group files have a file extension of .GRP and store information about which applications are contained within each group icon in the Program Manager.

Three categories of font files are associated with Windows 3.*x*: raster fonts, vector fonts, and printer fonts.

- *Raster fonts* are also known as bitmap fonts and are designed pixel by pixel. Since this type of font cannot be varied in size without being distorted, it requires a separate font file for each size and typeface you want to use.

- *Vector fonts* are also known as scaleable fonts. TrueType fonts are the new fonts used in Windows 3.*x*—they are similar to vector fonts, but are faster, more scaleable, and device independent. These fonts are stored as a series of points and mathematical formulas that can be re-created in any size or typeface.

- *Printer fonts* are contained in files that give the printer the proper instructions needed to construct the size and typeface. Printer fonts come in three types: device fonts, printable screen fonts, and soft fonts.

  - *Device fonts* are the fastest fonts to use since they are usually hard wired into the printer or inserted as a removable cartridge.

  - *Printable screen fonts* are the fonts used to display text on the screen. Windows converts these into printer fonts that the printer is able to use. Printing with these fonts increases print time due to the resources required for the conversion process.

  - *Soft fonts* are fonts that are downloaded from a disk or CD-ROM into either the printer's or the system's user memory.

Windows 95

Windows 95 has improved versions of many of the same system and user-interface files inherent in DOS and Windows 3.*x*, such as the IO.SYS, MSDOS.SYS, COMMAND.COM, .DLL, .INI, and program-accessory files. In addition, if you use legacy programs (programs designed for DOS or Windows 3.*x*), you will also have CONFIG.SYS, WIN.INI, AUTOEXEC.BAT, and SYSTEM.INI. Most of the functions of these last four files have been taken over by the Windows 95 Registry. The files particular to Windows 95 are as follows:

Registry: The Registry is a database used to store configuration information for both hardware and software components used by the system, devices, and applications.

Hardware tree: The hardware tree is another system database. It stores information generated by the Configuration Manager. This information is loaded into memory when the system boots and gives the system a description of current system settings.

INF files: These files are information files used when installing programs.

Application Programming Interface (API) files: APIs are used by the system to make hardware and software take notice of events that occur during program execution. An *event* is a change to current system settings. APIs contain a set of rules that govern what the operating system can do for an application. These rules are more important to programmers than to users since all applications must abide by these rules to work effectively in the Windows 95 environment.

Configuration Manager: The Configuration Manager is the major-domo for PnP services. It molds the hardware configuration for the system into the Registry database and assigns resources such as IRQs, DMAs, and port addresses to active device drivers.

Folder: A folder is a container that holds documents, applications, or subfolders.

Explorer: Explorer displays all the files and folders in one split window and lets you launch programs, locate specific files, and traverse the directory structure for all available drives.

Taskbar: The Taskbar acts as a placeholder for active folders, applications, and documents.

Start menu: The Start menu button is the place from where most applications are launched.

Recycle Bin: The Recycle Bin allows easy recovery of deleted files. To permanently eliminate a deleted file and free up the disk space, the Recycle Bin needs to be emptied.

My Computer folder: My Computer does the same basic things as Explorer, but instead of confining everything in one window, it opens a new window for every device or folder you double-click. Double-click the My Computer icon to display the disk drives, the Control Panel, and the Printer. If you double-click a disk drive, it will display the contents of the drive. If you right-click a disk drive, you can select the Properties option from the drop-down menu to see how much disk space is still available on that drive.

Control Panel: The Control Panel is used to set system parameters, add/remove software and hardware, set display options, and set network configuration.

Exam Essentials

The A+ exam measures your proficiency with and knowledge of the DOS, Windows 3.*x*, and Windows 95 operating environments. To repair a system, you must have a general knowledge of with what and how the operating system works and be able to navigate through the various elements of an operating system. Since an in-depth coverage of this material is beyond the scope of this book, a checklist of the basic skills you will need to be an A+ Service Technician is provided. It is crucial that you master the skills listed below.

SEE ALSO For detailed coverage of these skills, refer to *A+: Windows/DOS Study Guide* by David Groth, published by Sybex.

Make sure you are especially well grounded in the following topics for each of the operating environments:

- The functions and processes of each of the operating systems

- The major components of the operating systems: what they are used for, how they are utilized, and how they interact with each other

- The major system files: what they are, what they do, the order in which they are activated, and where they are located

- The commands that are most often used in CONFIG.SYS and AUTOEXEC.BAT, any default values for these commands, and commonly used switches

Know the primary functions of DOS.   The primary functions of DOS are to manage system resources, manage disk I/O, manage files, and execute programs.

Be familiar with the major elements of DOS.   DOS interacts with the user through COMMAND.COM, which contains the internal system commands and displays the DOS prompt on the command line. The prompt tells the user the currently active file (e.g., C:) and that the system is ready for use.

DOS interacts with the hardware through the ROM BIOS, which controls the hardware interfaces of the computer system. The BIOS is located in a set of chips on the motherboard and contains code hard wired into it at the factory. All requests to access hardware and all responses from the hardware pass through the BIOS.

The major portion of the operating system is contained in the IO.SYS and MSDOS.SYS files that are loaded at the end of the POST sequence by the boot loader.

The CONFIG.SYS and AUTOEXEC.BAT files accomplish custom configuration of the system. CONFIG.SYS is normally used to set up hardware drivers and activate TSR programs. AUTOEXEC.BAT is normally used to configure display, search drive paths, and automatically activate programs at boot up.

Know the primary functions of Windows 3.*x*.   The primary functions of Windows 3.*x* are to provide a user-friendly interface, run applications in a multi-tasking environment, manage files within the multi-tasking environment, and provide printing services for Windows-based applications.

Be familiar with the major components of the Windows 3.*x* environment.   The major components of Windows 3.*x* are system files and user-interface files.

The system files include WIN.COM, WIN.INI, and SYSTEM.INI, which activate and configure the GUI for the system. Other system files include USER.EXE, GDI.EXE, and KRNL*xxx*.EXE, which are core system files that control user input, graphic display, and system resources respectively.

The user-interface files include Program Manager, File Manager, Print Manager, and Control Panel. These programs present the Windows environment, assist users in navigating and managing the directory tree, control print jobs from Windows-based applications, and set the environment to user preferences respectively.

Know the basic elements of the Windows display (e.g., types and components of windows and menus). The major elements of the Windows display are the desktop, windows, icons, menus, dialog boxes, and the pointer.

The DLL files are core modules of programming code that are shared by several different applications. These dynamic link libraries allow programs to link into them and use them as part of their own program code.

Know the primary functions of Windows 95. The primary functions of Windows 95 are to manage system resources, manage disk I/O, manage files, and execute programs in a user-friendly interface within a multi-tasking, Plug-and-Play environment.

Be familiar with the major components of the Windows 95 environment. The major components of Windows 95 are the same as those for Windows 3.*x*, although they are much more versatile.

The system files include WIN.COM, WIN.INI, and SYSTEM.INI, which activate and configure the GUI for the system. Other system files include USER.EXE, GDI.EXE, and KRNL*xxx*.EXE, which are core system files that control user input, graphic display, and system resources respectively.

The user-interface files include Program Manager, File Manager, Print Manager, and Control Panel. These programs present the Windows environment, assist users in navigating and managing the directory tree, control print jobs from Windows-based applications, and set the environment to user preferences respectively.

Know the basic elements of the Windows 95 display (e.g., types and components of windows and menus). The major elements of the Windows 95 display are the same as with Windows 3.*x* except that Windows 95 has a few additional elements.

A *folder* is a container that holds documents, applications, or subfolders. *Explorer* displays all the files and folders in one split window and lets you launch programs, locate specific files, and traverse the directory structure for all available drives. The *Taskbar* acts as a placeholder for active folders, applications, and documents. The *Start menu button* is the place from where most applications are launched. The *Recycle Bin* allows easy recovery of deleted files. To permanently eliminate a deleted file and free up the disk space, the Recycle Bin needs to be emptied. *My Computer* opens a new window for every device or folder you double-click. It displays the disk drives, the Control Panel, and the Printer. The *Control Panel* is used to set system parameters, add/remove software, add/remove hardware, set display options, and set network configuration.

Key Terms and Concepts

ASCII (American Standard Code for Information Interchange):   A numerical code system used to represent characters on a PC. Usually it is synonymous with a text file.

Associate: When used in a Windows context, it means to connect a file with a specific file extension (e.g., .DOC) with a certain program (e.g., MS Word).

Attribute: A bit attached to a file header that determines how the system treats the file. Four different types of attributes can be assigned to a file. A file can contain none or all of the attributes. The attributes are Read Only (R), Archive (A), System (S), and Hidden (H). With Windows 95, you can also set attributes for folders.

Bootable disk: A diskette containing the system files needed for booting up the computer. Should also contain AUTOEXEC.BAT, CONFIG.SYS, and drivers for other devices such as a CD-ROM drive.

Configuration: The set values for a device or system that determine the device's default parameters.

Cooperative multi-tasking: A feature of an operating system that allows it to run more than one task or application at a time. In cooperative multi-tasking, the applications are responsible for the use of system resources. If one application crashes without releasing the resources it has control over, the entire system locks up, usually requiring a system reboot. This is the type of multi-tasking used with Windows 3.*x* and its applications.

Default: The configuration settings initially set by the system or changed by the user that will automatically take effect when the device is activated.

Dialog box: A small window used by the system to get additional information from a user.

Document-centric: This concept is new to Windows 95. It gives the user a more real-world view of the information in the computer as well as a more readily understood concept of working with it. There are two basic features of this approach: the file system (directory tree) is organized into folders that can contain files or other folders; by selecting a particular document, you can launch the program that created it automatically.

Driver: A program that is device specific. It optimizes the device for use with the system.

Dynamic link library (DLL):   A file that contains program code needed by multiple applications.

External commands: These are the DOS commands located as files in the DOS directory on the hard disk drive. They are external to COMMAND.COM and have to be loaded into memory each time they are called.

Folder: The document-centric method for storing and organizing files. It is synonymous with the directory in DOS-based file structures.

Initialize: To prepare for use. Program files are initialized as they are launched. Disks are initialized by formatting them. In programming, it is the process of returning everything to a known state or value.

Internal commands: In the DOS realm, these commands are the ones present in memory while the operating system is active. You will not find these commands located as files on the hard disk drive. These commands are internal to the COMMAND.COM file.

Preemptive multi-tasking: A feature of an operating system that allows it to run more than one application at a time. In this type of multi-tasking, the operating system retains control over system resources and allocates them to each active application on an on-demand, time-slice basis. If one application crashes, the system restores itself at the end of the allocated time period and continues to function. This is the type of multi-tasking used with Windows 95 applications.

Protocol: A set of rules that governs how data are sent and received between devices.

Registry: The Registry is a database of system resources. It contains all of the configuration information for the computer and its network setup as well as the user's current session information on the computer.

System resources: Usually refers to the amount of memory in a computer system, but it also applies to the IRQs, DMAs, and storage space on the system.

Sample Questions

1. In what sequence does DOS load its system files during the boot-up process?

   A. MSDOS.SYS, IO.SYS, COMMAND.COM, CONFIG.SYS

   B. IO.SYS, MSDOS.SYS, CONFIG.SYS, COMMAND.COM

   C. IO.SYS, MSDOS.SYS, AUTOEXEC.BAT, COMMAND.COM

   D. IO.SYS, MSDOS.SYS, COMMAND.COM, AUTOEXEC.BAT

   Answer: B, D. If all files are present, the boot sequence that DOS follows is IO.SYS, MSDOS.SYS, CONFIG.SYS, COMMAND.COM, and AUTOEXEC.BAT, but the AUTOEXEC.BAT and CONFIG.SYS files are optional.

2. What are the two files used by Windows 95 to develop the Registry?

   A. USER.DAT

   B. GDI.DAT

   C. SYSTEM.DAT

   D. IO.SYS

Answer: A, C. The USER.DAT file contains information on the user(s); the SYSTEM.DAT file holds information on the system configuration.

Identify ways to navigate the operating system and how to get to needed technical information.

This objective focuses on the methods and procedures the operating systems use to locate and access files, and on how to use the online help features. You will need to know the following material for the exam:

- How DOS/Windows 3.x and Windows 95 organize and display their directory trees

- How to use DOS command-line strings to get from one branch of the directory tree to another; create relative and absolute path names; use path names in command-line strings to retrieve data, launch programs, etc.; and use the FIND command to locate files with specific information in them

- How to use Windows 3.x File Manager and Windows 95 Explorer to display directory structure, search for and locate specific files, access and retrieve data from files, and launch program applications directly or through associations

A well-grounded knowledge in these areas will help you design a workable data structure for your system, efficiently locate specific files, and move around in the operating systems' environments.

Critical Information

DOS and Windows 95 organize their files in directories set up in a hierarchical manner. This parent-child relationship is such that each child directory has only one parent directory. Each directory can contain other directories and/or files. See Figure 1.1 below.

F I G U R E 1.1: Typical hierarchical directory tree

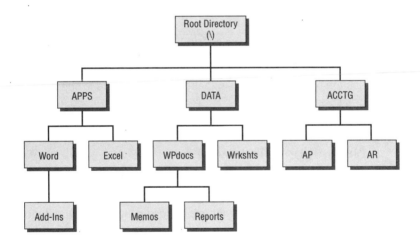

The directory structure is referred to as a directory tree with the *root* directory at the top of the tree and each directory off the root referred to as a *branch*. Navigating the directory tree is a matter of going from a parent to one of its children to travel down the tree (or child to parent to travel up the tree), repeating the process as needed until you reach the destination directory.

Each operating-system environment has multiple ways in which to navigate its directory structure and retrieve files. In all of them, you can set up a *search path* using the PATH command in the AUTOEXEC.BAT file. This will allow the operating system to automatically look for a program in the directories listed in the PATH string.

Navigating DOS

DOS uses either the CD command at the command-line prompt or the DOSSHELL menu utility. With DOS, you must be familiar with how the directory tree is constructed to create the appropriate path for a directory location or path name for a file. (A *path name* consists of the path through the directory plus the filename.) If you are not familiar with the directory tree, you can use the TREE command to get a screen layout of the structure.

TIP When using the TREE command, it is best to pipe it into the MORE command to vertically scroll through the display. Otherwise, use the pause switch (/S) with the TREE command to see the display one screen at a time.

Navigating Windows 3.x

Windows 3.x uses the File Manager to move between branches of the directory tree; or, you can set up group directories in the Program Manager that contain either programs or documents. When you double-click a program icon, it will launch the program. If you double-click a document icon, it will launch its associated program with the document already open, or it will display a list of applications from which you may choose the program you want to associate with the document.

Navigating Windows 95

Windows 95 uses either Explorer or My Computer to navigate through the directory structure. Explorer is document oriented and, like the File Manager, displays everything in a single window. My Computer is device oriented and will display a new window for every icon you double-click.

Help Features in DOS, Windows 3.x, and Windows 95

DOS, Windows 3.*x*, and Windows 95 all have their own built-in help features. DOS uses the HELP command at the DOS prompt, a command followed by /?, or a menu option on the menu bar of DOS-SHELL. Windows 3.*x* and Windows 95 have a Help option on their menu bars. Both have context-sensitive features, but Windows 95 is much more sophisticated in its ability to help you.

Necessary Procedures

Knowing how to get around the directory tree and locate files is essential to working with any operating system. You should be familiar with the procedures discussed in this section.

Navigating a Directory Tree in DOS

The following procedure is the means by which you can move around a DOS-based directory structure by using DOS commands at the prompt.

1. The CD command is used to change directories. The syntax is as follows:

   `C:\> CD path\filename`

2. Paths can be either *absolute*, which means the path starts at the root (top-most) directory, or *relative*, which means it starts from the current active directory. Any path name that starts with a backslash (\ ) is an absolute path name. If it starts with anything else, it is a relative path name.

   - Example 1—the *absolute* path name:

     `C:\> CD c:\APPS\WORD`

   - Example 2—the *relative* path name:

     `C:\> CD WORD`

3. Both commands take you to the same subdirectory (WORD), but only the absolute path name can be used to get you there from anywhere in the directory. The relative path name gets to the WORD directory only if you are in the APPS directory.

4. Once you have reached the directory you want, you can display the file list (DIR), copy files to other directories (COPY), rename files (REN), move files to other directories (MOVE), delete files (DEL), view the contents of an ASCII file (TYPE), or launch programs by entering their name at the command prompt.

Navigating a Directory Tree Using DOSSHELL

The DOSSHELL is a user-friendly means of navigating a DOS-based directory with a menu system.

1. Open DOSSHELL by typing **DOSSHELL** at the command prompt.

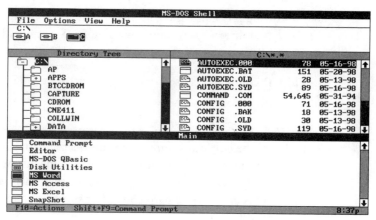

2. Once the display screen is active, you can use the mouse or keyboard to navigate the menu to change directories, manipulate files, and launch programs.

3. To exit the DOSSHELL, select File ➤ Exit.

Navigating a Directory Tree with the Windows 3.*x* File Manager

Windows 3.*x* comes with its own GUI-based utility. The File Manager can be used to navigate the entire file system of the computer and perform file-management tasks along the way.

1. Open Windows by typing **WIN** at the command prompt or by inserting WIN as the last line in your AUTOEXEC.BAT file.

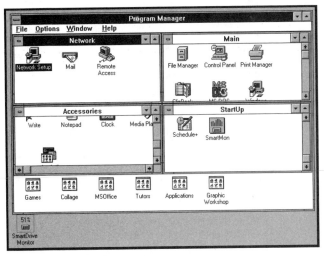

2. Once the Windows Program Manager is open, you can use the mouse to double-click the group icons to open them up to display their program icons. If you double-click a program icon, it will launch the program. You can also use the File option on the menu bar to manipulate files as needed.

3. To navigate the directory structure, double-click the group icon for MAIN in the Program Manager and then double-click the File Manager icon.

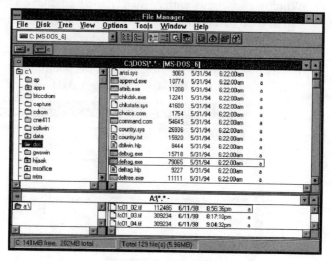

4. To exit File Manager, double-click the control box in the upper-left corner. To exit Windows, choose File ➤ Exit or double-click the control box.

Navigating a File System with the Start Menu in Windows 95

The Start menu is a shortcut method for gaining access to your files. With it, you can launch applications, get help, locate files, set environment values, and shut down your system.

1. To open the Start menu, click the Start button on the Taskbar.

2. Select the menu option you need—the associated files and sub-folders will appear in pop-up menus.

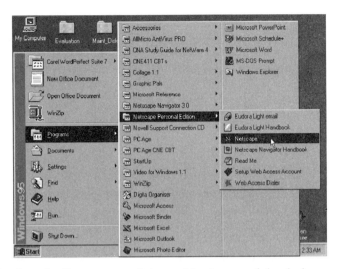

3. To close the Start menu, click any blank area of the desktop.

Navigating a File System with Windows Explorer

The Windows Explorer is a more file- and directory-oriented utility. This method closely resembles the features found in the Windows 3.*x* File Manager.

1. To activate the Windows Explorer, click the Start button on the Taskbar, click the Programs option, and then click Windows Explorer.

2. Once in Explorer, you can select the disk drive, folder, and files with which you need to work. If you do not know where a file is located, you can use the FIND option to locate it. Everything in the Explorer is displayed in a single screen.

3. You can exit Explorer by clicking the "X" box in the upper-right corner of the window.

Navigating a File System with My Computer in Windows 95

Another way to travel through the file system is to use the My Computer icon on the desktop.

1. Double-click My Computer, then the disk drive you want to work with, and finally the subsequent folders until you reach your destination.

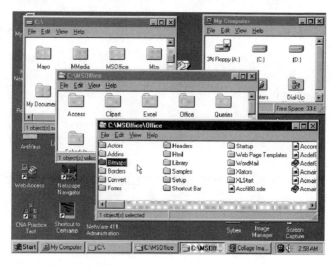

2. Close all unnecessary folders to conserve memory resources by clicking the "X" box in the upper-right corner of the title bar.

3. Expand the destination window to full screen by clicking the Maximize button in the upper-right portion of the title bar.

4. To take the folder back to its original size, click the Restore button next to the Maximize button. You can also send the window down to the Taskbar by clicking the underscore (_) button on the title bar.

Exam Essentials

To master this area of the exam, you should have an in-depth knowledge of the following areas.

Know the methods used by DOS to locate, access, and retrieve data files.   DOS uses either the command-line prompt or DOS-SHELL to locate, access, and retrieve data. To use the command line, you must know the correct syntax for constructing a path name that will properly reference the directory you wish to access. To use DOS-SHELL, you need to set up the menu to reflect the way you wish to access applications. You should be very knowledgeable with the command-line path names and familiar with DOSSHELL.

Know the methods Windows 3.x uses to locate, access, and retrieve files.   Windows 3.x extensively uses the File Manager to accomplish these tasks. You can also use the File option in Program Manager, select the Run option, or double-click an application icon to launch programs. If a program is associated with a particular document type (determined by the file extension), double-clicking the document icon will launch the program and load the file into the document window. You should have an in-depth knowledge of the functions available in File Manager.

Know the methods Windows 95 uses to locate, access, and retrieve files.   Windows 95 uses Microsoft Explorer and My Computer to navigate the file system. Explorer contains all of its displays within the same window, while My Computer spreads open folders all over the face of the desktop. Explorer is more document oriented and displays its directory structure as folders within the file system. My Computer starts with devices that display folders or files in separate windows without giving any idea of the overall file structure set up on the disk drive.

Key Terms and Concepts

Active window: The open window you are currently using. The pointer and keyboard will affect this window. The title bar is usually a brighter color than the other windows.

Application: A set of programs that perform a given task such as word processing, database management, etc.

Associate: The process of linking a file extension with a particular application. Once associated, if you double-click a file with an associated extension, the application will be launched automatically and the document will be loaded into the application.

Background: The portion of the desktop behind the active screen. A utility or an application, other than the active window, running in memory. Examples include TSRs and print spoolers.

Current path: The path from the root to the current directory. Also used to refer to the order in which DOS will access search drives for a file based on the entries of the PATH statement in AUTOEXEC.BAT.

File extension: The optional one to three characters on a filename. If used, there is a period between the filename and the file extension.

Filename: The name given to any file stored on the hard disk. DOS filenames are from two to eight characters long. Windows 95 may have from one to 255 characters in a filename.

Folder: The method used by Windows 95 to organize its files on the directory tree. Folders are the same as directories in DOS/ Windows 3.*x*.

Path: The location of a file on the disk. The absolute path refers to the location from the root directory. The relative path refers to the location from another location on the directory tree other than the root directory.

Path name: The name of a file (and extension) preceded by the path to the file.

Plug and Play (PnP): A newer standard for hardware that allows installation of the hardware onto a system with little or no assistance from the user. PnP is common in Windows 95 systems.

Program groups: Refers to the group icons on the Windows 3.*x* Program Manager screen. These groups contain other icons usually associated with a particular application or user.

Program Manager: The initial screen for Windows 3.*x* that is the base for all other operations. It contains the menus that will open other devices and the group icons that contain all the program and document icons.

Switches: Options for command-line entries that modify the command's actions or tailor it to a more specific need.

Wildcard characters: Characters used to specify a single character (?) or an all-inclusive group of characters (*). These characters are needed when working with multiple files with which you want to do the same thing to all of them at the same time.

Window: A rectangular area on the desktop that displays either the functions of the application (application window) or the contents of a file (document window).

Sample Questions

1. You are in the C:\ directory and need to delete all the files on the A: drive. Which of the following commands would you use?

   A. Del ?.?

   B. Del *.*

   C. Del a:*.*

   D. Del a:\?.?

   Answer: C. Choice B would delete all files in the current directory (C:\). By using the drive specifier, you tell the operating system you want the command for the A: drive.

2. How many characters can you have in a path name for Windows 95?

   A. 8

   B. 3

   C. 255

   D. 260

   Answer: D. Choice C is the number of characters in a complete path name that includes folders and subfolders.

Identify basic concepts and procedures for creating, viewing, and managing files and directories, including procedures for changing file attributes and the ramifications of changes (for example, security issues).

This objective concentrates on the syntax used with commands, file types, and file-naming conventions, and the use of the ATTRIB command and the results associated with setting a file's attributes. You will have to know the following subjects for this objective:

- How to construct command strings using proper syntax

- How to name files in both DOS and Windows 95

- How to determine the different file types and formats available, and what they do

- How to determine what ramifications can occur from changing the attributes of a file

- How to use the DOS ATTRIB command to change a file's attributes

- How to use the File Manager in Windows 3.*x* to change attributes
- How to use the right-click pop-up menu to change file attributes in Windows 95

Critical Information

Both the DOS/Windows 3.*x* and the Windows 95 environments place restrictions on file-naming conventions. Windows 95 is much more liberal than DOS, but it still has restrictions that must be followed.

Classification of Files by Type and Format

There are several ways to classify the different types of files used by the operating systems. Files can be differentiated as being either binary or ASCII, or they can be classified as program, system, or data files.

File formats: The type of format the file's content is in can be used to classify a file. There are two types of file formats:

- **Binary:** Binary files are files whose contents are in a machine-readable format of ones and zeros. These can be either executable files or application data files.

- **ASCII:** ASCII files are text files that can be easily read with a text editor or the TYPE command. They consist of the alphanumeric characters assigned by the American Standard Code for Information Interchange.

File types: Files can also be classified according to their purpose and use. There are three basic categories in this classification:

- **Application:** Application files are binary executable files such as word processors, spreadsheets, and database managers.

- **Data:** Data files can be either ASCII or binary. They contain data placed there by the system or an application. Examples include document files from applications and information files from system activities.

- **System:** System files can be either ASCII or binary. Most, by far, are binary. These files make up the operating system and the utilities that come with it. ASCII system files include CONFIG.SYS, AUTOEXEC.BAT, WIN.INI, and SYSTEM.INI. Binary system files include the kernel, COMMAND.COM, WIN.COM, and utilities such DEFRAG and SCANDISK.

File Naming in DOS and Windows 3.x

In DOS and Windows 3.x, filenames must follow the 8.3 rule and must not use selected character symbols. This rule specifies that files can have names from one to eight characters long, and if you use an extension on the file, it can have from one to three characters.

- Filenames can start with a character or number and contain any combinations of characters and numbers as long as you don't exceed eight of them. File extensions can be any combination of characters and numbers as long as you don't exceed three.

- A period is used to separate the filename from the optional file extension, if one is used.

- Filenames and extensions can be either upper- or lowercase.

- Filenames cannot contain a space or use the following symbols: comma (,), wedges (< >), question mark (?), forward and backward slashes (/ \), colon (:), vertical bar (|), semicolon (;), quotation marks ("″), apostrophes ("), square brackets ([ ]), plus sign (+), or equal sign (=).

File Naming in Windows 95

Windows 95 supports the long-filename convention. The rules are as follows:

- You can use up to 255 characters in a filename. Keep in mind, though, the path name to include folders, subfolders, and filename cannot exceed 260 characters.

- You can include a space in the filename and have multiple periods in it.

- The number of symbols that you cannot use has been shortened to the following ones: forward and backward slashes (/ \), asterisk (*), wedges (< >), colon (:), question mark (?), quotation marks (" "), and vertical bar (|).

- You can use the comma (,), semicolon (;), equal sign (=), and square brackets ([ ]) in filenames.

When these long filenames are used in a DOS-based system, the long filename is converted to the DOS 8.3 rule. Usually this involves taking the first six characters of the filename and appending a tilde (~) and numeric value to the shortened filename. The numbers are assigned according to the date and time the file was created.

NOTE   Both DOS and Windows 95 support the use of wildcards. The asterisk (*) is used to replace multiple characters, and the question mark (?) is used to replace a single character.

Changing File Attributes

DOS, Windows 3.*x*, and Windows 95 all have their own way in which to change a file's attributes.

In DOS, you use the ATTRIB command at the DOS prompt as follows:

- The plus (+) turns on an attribute, and the minus (–) turns it off.

- The R attribute is Read Only. When set, files can only be read.

- The A attribute is Archive. It indicates the file has been changed.

- The S attribute is System. It marks the file for the operating system.

- The H attribute is Hidden. It hides and protects the file.

Windows 3.1 takes a GUI approach using the File Manager. To view a file's attributes, you use the View option in the File Manager. To set the attributes, you must choose File ➤ Properties.

To set attributes in Windows 95, you right-click any file or folder icon and select Properties from the pop-up menu. In the Properties page, you click the boxes next to the attributes you want to activate for the object. Windows 95 allows you to place attributes on folders as well as individual files.

Knowing what the attributes do is of critical importance. A file's attributes determine how the operating system treats it, how applications relate with it, and how your backup system uses it. In addition, attributes set the file's security issues and determine what a user can do with the file.

- The *Read Only* attribute affects the file's ability to be manipulated. When turned on, the file may be read, but cannot be modified, renamed, or deleted.

- The *Archive* attribute lets the system know whether the file has been changed in any way. Backup systems rely on this attribute when they do an incremental backup.

- The *System* attribute marks the file as a system file set aside for use by the operating system. This attribute is available only in versions of DOS 5 and later.

- The *Hidden* attribute affects the way in which the file can be displayed. When this attribute is set, the file cannot be displayed with a normal DIR command, and the file cannot be copied, renamed, or deleted.

Necessary Procedures

Learn the following procedures thoroughly. They will be invaluable when setting up systems that need particular tuning for security, backup, and access control.

Setting the File Attributes in DOS with the ATTRIB Command

The ATTRIB command is used quite a bit in file management. You will need to know how to set and unset the different attributes to do your work.

1. Change to the directory the file is in.

2. Type in the command string with the attributes as needed. For example, to change a single attribute for a single file, type **C:\DATA\> ATTRIB +R MYFILE.TXT**. To change multiple attributes for a single file, type **C:\DATA\> ATTRIB +R +A +H MYFILE.TXT**. To change a single attribute for an entire directory and subdirectories, type **C:\DATA\> ATTRIB +R *.* /S**.

3. To view the attributes for the files in a directory, use the ATTRIB command by itself.

Setting the File Attributes in Windows 3.*x*

Setting a file's attributes in Windows 3.*x* is easier than in DOS due to the GUI characteristics of the File Manager.

1. Open the File Manager.

2. To view the current settings for a file, highlight the file and choose View ➤ All File Details.

3. To change a file's attributes, highlight the file and choose File ➤ Properties.

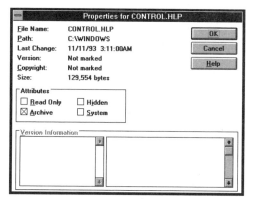

4. Click the checkboxes for the attributes you wish to change. If attributes have a check in their box, it indicates they have already been applied.

5. Click the OK button to exit the Properties page.

Setting the File Attributes in Windows 95

Setting the file attributes in Windows 95 is as simple as clicking an icon.

1. Right-click the file whose attributes you wish to change to display a drop-down menu.

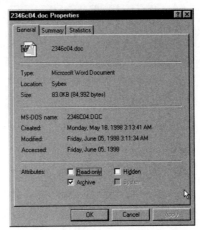

2. Click the Properties option to display the Properties page for the file.

3. Click the attributes listed on the General page you wish to add or remove. The active attributes have a check in the box.

4. Click OK to exit the Properties page.

Exam Essentials

Naming files is an essential part of working with both the DOS/Windows 3.*x* and the Windows 95 environments. Be sure you have a definite understanding of the different conventions used for each operating system and can use them without a lot of trouble.

Know which characters can be used with a DOS filename. In addition to the alpha-numeric characters, the only characters you can use in DOS/Windows 3.*x* are braces ({ }), underscore (_), hyphen (-), parentheses (()), asterisk (*), "and" symbol (&), caret (^), percent symbol (%), dollar sign ($), pound (#), and "at" symbol (@).

Know which characters can be used with a Windows 95 filename. In addition to the alpha-numeric characters, the only characters you can use in Windows 95 are braces ({ }), underscore (_), hyphen (-), parentheses (()), asterisk (*), "and" symbol (&), caret (^), percent symbol (%), dollar sign ($), pound (#), "at" symbol (@), square brackets ([ ]), comma (,), semicolon (;), equal sign (=), and the space.

Be able to recognize and create proper filenames.   DOS requires you to use the 8.3 rule. You can use up to eight characters for the filename and up to three characters for the file extension. Windows 95 can have a maximum of 255 characters in a filename, but only 260 characters in the complete path name.

Know what happens when you use a Windows 95 long filename in a DOS program or use a DOS-based utility to work with your files.   DOS converts the long filename into an abbreviated filename that follows the 8.3 rule. In most cases, the long filename is truncated to the first four characters you used in the long filename, and a tilde (~) and numerical sequence are appended to the abbreviated name. The numeric sequence is based on the creation date/time of the file and not on any numbering system you may have used in naming the file to begin with.

Know how each of the attributes affects a file.   The R attribute sets the file to Read Only. When this attribute is set, the file cannot be modified or erased. The A attribute sets the file's Archive bit, which indicates the file has been modified since it was last backed up. The S attribute marks the file as a system file that needs special consideration and action from the operating system. The H attribute hides the file from normal browsers such as the DIR command, and keeps the file from being deleted or copied.

Know how to use DOS, Windows 3.x, and Windows 95 to change file attributes.   To change the file attributes in DOS, you must use the ATTRIB command with the appropriate attribute—Read Only, Archive, System, and Hidden. Multiple attributes may be set on the same command line, but each attribute and its associated on/off flag must be separated with a space on the command line. To change an attribute in Windows 3.x, you choose File ➤ Properties to display the Properties page. With Windows 95, you can change a file's attributes by right-clicking after you have highlighted the file's icon. Attributes are then changed on the Properties page.

Know how to use DOS, Windows 3.*x*, and Windows 95 to view file attributes. To view the attributes for files in a directory in DOS, use the ATTRIB command by itself. To view the attributes for a file in Windows 3.*x*, choose View ➤ Properties while in File Manager. In Windows 95, you can view a file's attributes by selecting the Properties option to display the Properties page.

Key Terms and Concepts

Archive: An attribute used to mark a file for backup. It indicates the file has been modified since the last backup was made.

ASCII text file: A simple data file that is made up of ASCII characters and can be viewed with the TYPE command, the DOS editor, or Windows Notepad.

ATTRIB: The DOS command used to change a file's attributes.

Attribute: The unique features of a file that determine how the operating system accesses and manipulates the file.

Backup: The process used to make a duplicate of the file system for system protection. There are full backups, incremental backups, and differential backups.

Current path: The sequence of parent-to-child relationships that exists from the root directory to the present location in the directory tree.

Device files: Files that usually end in .SYS. A device file is used to control a specific device such as the monitor, keyboard, memory, or printer so that the full features of the device can be used in the system. Also referred to as drivers.

Dynamic link library files: Files with information or instructions needed by applications. Both Windows 3.*x* and Windows 95 rely heavily on these files for their operation.

Extension: The optional part of a filename that follows the period. It can be from one to three characters in size. Many applications use the extension to recognize data files that belong to them.

File: A means of storing different kinds of things on the storage media. There are several different types of files. Major groupings of files can be done by determining if they are executable or data files. Another way of classifying files is by the type of data in them, either binary or ASCII text.

Font: The typeface of a character. It determines its shape, style, and size and has names such as Arial and Times New Roman.

Font files: Files that contain a kind of typeface used with either printers or screen displays. There are four basic types of font files: raster or bitmapped fonts, vector fonts, printer fonts, and screen fonts.

Group files: Windows files that have a file extension of .GRP. These files contain information about the different groups you have set up in your Windows 3.*x* Program Manager.

Hidden attribute: The attribute that hides the file from regular browsers and prevents the file from being copied or deleted.

Path: The location of the file within the directory tree. It is composed of the logical drive letter on which the file resides and all the levels of directories in which the file is contained.

PostScript fonts: Proprietary vector fonts that require special device drivers or printers to handle them. They are used extensively in laser printers.

Printable screen fonts: Typefaces that can be used with either screen displays or hardcopy printer output.

Printer fonts: Typefaces used primarily for printer output.

Program information files: Windows files with an extension of .PIF. These files are used to optimize DOS-based programs to work within the Windows environment.

Program initialization files: Windows files that have a .INI file extension. These files are usually loaded as part of an application and contain information the program needs for initial start-up.

Raster fonts or graphics: Fonts that are created by bitmapping the image. The image is created pixel by pixel. For fonts, each font size is stored in a separate file. Raster images do not resize very well. Resizing gives them a jagged appearance. These fonts are also called nonscaleable and bitmapped fonts.

Read Only: A file attribute that prevents the file from being modified, deleted, or overwritten. It also prevents the file from being renamed, though it can be copied.

Screen fonts: Typefaces used primarily for screen display.

Sections: The divisions used to group information in an INI file.

Shortcut file: A Windows 95 feature that allows you to place an icon for a file anywhere in the system without having to copy the file. A shortcut icon is a link that points to the actual location of the file in the directory.

Swap file: A pseudo file used to reserve space on the hard drive for its virtual-memory feature. Programs are switched in and out of memory, and out of and onto the hard disk swap-file area.

Switches: Command-line options used with most DOS commands to invoke special features built into the command.

System: A file attribute that marks the file for system use. It tells the operating system that the file is needed by the operating system. Prevents the file from being deleted.

TrueType fonts: Vector fonts that are printable screen fonts. They are used extensively in Windows and Macintosh screen displays. They have a true WYSIWYG display characteristic.

Vector fonts: Fonts that are created using set reference points and mathematical models. These fonts can be easily resized and retain their same features. These fonts are also known as scaleable fonts.

Sample Questions

1. Which of the following is an example of a good filename in DOS?

   A. DataFile01.dbf

   B. Report.Jan97

C. Inven_10.97

D. Exam File.T2

Answer: C. The other responses have either too many characters in the name or extension, or contain illegal characters.

2. Which of the following is an example of a good filename in Windows 95?

A. DataFile01.dbf

B. Report.Jan97

C. Inven_10.97

D. Exam File.T2

Answer: A, B, C, D. Windows 95 is more flexible on its naming conventions and supports the long-filename standard.

3. Which property allows you to keep the file from being copied and deleted?

A. Read Only

B. System

C. Archive

D. Hidden

Answer: D. The Hidden attribute not only hides the file from normal browsers, it also keeps the file from being copied or deleted.

4. Which attribute is used with backup systems?

A. Read Only

B. System

C. Archive

D. Hidden

Answer: C. The Archive bit is turned whenever the file is backed up. When the file is modified after the backup, the attribute is turned on. It is used extensively for incremental backups.

Identify the procedures for basic disk management.

This section deals with the ways in which the operating systems store data on the hard disk drive, and the procedures, utilities, and methods used to get a disk drive ready for use, including optimizing its performance, checking it for bad sectors, and backing up the file system. This section requires a knowledge of the following items:

- The method the operating systems use for storing the file index

- What the FATs are and where they are located

- The difference between the way DOS/Windows 3.*x* and Windows 95 store their FATs

- Disk management strategies and utilities

- Backup strategies and utilities

- Preparation of a disk drive using FDISK, FORMAT, etc.

- Optimizing disk performance with DEFRAG

- Using SCANDISK to isolate bad sectors

Critical Information

As a PC repair technician responsible for the continued operation of the PCs assigned to your care and the reduced downtime of inoperable systems, you need to devise a strategy for coping with problems before they occur. Prior planning always is worth the effort because things *will* go wrong—it's just a matter of time.

Your strategy should include preventive maintenance, periodic benchmark tests, scheduled periodic backup procedures, keeping mission-critical repair parts on hand, and reliable repair channels that can support your needs in your timetable.

The Basic Elements of Disk Storage

The hard drive consists of a number of disks or platters that spin at 3,500 rpm or higher. Each disk is divided into concentric circles called *tracks*, and each track is divided into segments called *sectors*. Sectors are numbered consecutively starting at sector 1. Both the top and the bottom of the platters are used for storage. A *cylinder* is comprised of the same track number on each disk (e.g., track 3 on all the disks, top and bottom, would be referred to as cylinder 3).

The outermost track is called track 0, and each track is incremented by one as you go toward the center of the disk. The top side of the top disk is called side 0, and the bottom is called side 1. The top of the next disk is called side 2, and its bottom side is called side 3.

When a hard drive is prepared for use, it must be partitioned and formatted. Partitioning the drive places information about the size and location of the partitions on the hard drive. The partition table occupies the first sector of the drive (cylinder 0, side 0, sector 1). Formatting the drive locates the tracks, sectors, and sides of the drive and records the information as an index in the drive's boot record. The boot record occupies the hard drive's second sector, and contains the files necessary for locating the operating system files and a loader program that loads them into memory. Formatting the drive also initializes the file allocation table (FAT).

Addressing physical locations on the hard drive is a matter of stating the cylinder number, the side number, and the sector number. For instance, the location for the third sector on the fourth track of the top side of the second platter would be referred to as cylinder 4, side 2, sector 4. These addresses are correlated to the logical addresses used by the operating system for storing data.

The File Allocation Table

The *FAT* is the index to your file system. It provides the operating system with the means to locate the files you want by cross referencing a filename to its physical location on the disk drive.

A firm understanding of this subject matter will go a long way in helping you determine that a problem is with the FAT, and will guide you in your attempts at repairing it without totally trashing the system.

The OS uses the FAT to keep track of the physical location of its files on the hard disk drive. It is the index to the files located on the disk. The FAT is created by the FORMAT command and is located on the first sector of the hard disk drive. There are usually two copies of the FAT in case one gets corrupted—the other can be used to restore integrity to the file structure.

- A *lost cluster* is a disk-storage area that is not claimed by any file, but has not been marked as released in the FAT.

- *Cross-linked files* are clusters that are marked in the FAT as belonging to more than one file.

- *Fragmented files* are files that have more than one physical location assigned to them in the FAT.

There are two basic types of FAT common to the PC world: FAT16 and FAT32.

- FAT16 is the type of FAT used with DOS and Windows 3.*x*. It is the original type of FAT and is based on a 16-bit block. This size limits both the size of the filenames and the number of entries that can be assigned to the root directory.

- VFAT, or virtual file allocation table, is a pseudo 32-bit FAT. VFAT sets aside a portion of the FAT for long filenames. This area is set aside for backward compatibility with DOS/Windows 3.*x* files.

NOTE There is also a true 32-bit FAT used with Windows NT that does not concern itself with backward compatibility with legacy programs.

DOS-based programs can damage the VFAT and destroy the area used for the long filename. The DOS utilities SCANDISK and

CHKDSK can virtually destroy your file system by converting all your entries for long filenames into the ~01 format, where the tilde (~) is the first six characters of the filename, and the 01 is a sequential numbering of files with the same characters. The sequence is based on the file creation date. Even a simple DEL command can leave the long-filename section of the VFAT untouched.

Disk Management Utilities

In the life of every system, there comes a time when things go wrong. Many times, the problem is with your hard disk drive. To resolve such problems, you need to know how to use the disk management utilities such as SCANDISK, CHKDSK, FDISK /MBR, and SYS. These utilities will help you overcome many of the problems associated with hard disk drives.

> **SCANDISK:** This utility is used to check your system for defects on the hard disk drive and block off sectors that are no longer usable. This utility should be run at least once a quarter (more if your PC has a lot of disk-based transactions) and whenever the drive starts to act strangely or loses data.

> **CHKDSK:** This is the legacy program for DOS. It checks the integrity of the files on the disk drive, and with the /F switch, it can "fix" files that have lost their end-of-file (EOF) flag. The files are converted to CHKDSK files (FILE0001.CSK) that can then be viewed and sorted back to their proper files. This process is too time consuming to consider seriously, but it does get rid of troublesome files. This sometimes requires a major reinstallation of an application or operating system if one of the major system files was "fixed" in this manner.

> **FDISK /MBR:** This utility is used to place a generic boot sector on the hard disk drive. If the system has trouble booting, this command may fix the problem. If you have a multiple-operating-system boot manager, it will be overwritten.

> **SYS:** This is used to restore the system files onto the disk. If your system boots from a floppy and recognizes the hard drive, this utility may fix the problem.

NOTE Third-party resources such as Norton Utilities, PCTools, RESCUE, and Drive Pro go much more deeply into disk management.

Necessary Procedures

Backing up your hard drive and keeping it working at optimal performance are critical parts of being a service technician. You should know what is involved in performing the following procedures.

Backing Up a Disk

Methods of backing up your system include the DOS BACKUP command, Windows 3.*x* MSBACKUP, and Windows 95 MSBACKUP. The DOS BACKUP command is archaic and slow as molasses. Starting with DOS 6, MSBACKUP is much more reliable, faster, and more user friendly.

BACKUP: This command simply copies the designated files and directories to another medium (usually floppy disks) in a compressed format. With today's large disk drives, you'll spend a fortune on floppies. To restore the backup files onto your hard drive, you need the RESTORE command.

MSBACKUP: This is a condensed version of a famous third-party vendor. It replaces both the BACKUP and RESTORE commands. It is a menu-driven utility that makes selection a lot simpler than with the DOS command. MSBACKUP works with both Windows 3.*x* and Windows 95.

There are three basic types of backup: full, incremental, and differential.

- *Full backup* takes the longest because it backs up all the files on the system or that part of the system you have designated for backup. This backup method sets the Archive bit on to indicate to the backup utility that the file is already archived.

- *Incremental backup* is the fastest backup method since it backs up only those files that have been modified since the last full and/or incremental backup. This method also sets the Archive bit on.

- *Differential backups* cannot be performed by the utilities supplied by the operating system. This method does not take as long as a full backup, but is not as fast as an incremental backup. This method does not reset the Archive bit one way or the other. It does not check the Archive bit, but backs up all files except those that have not been changed since the last full backup, regardless of any incremental backups that may have been performed since then.

NOTE   With the size of the hard disk drive being placed in PCs, a tape backup system is almost mandatory, although with the lowering prices of recordable CD-ROM drives, these devices may become more popular as backup devices. At this time, though, tape drives are the most economical in price and storage media.

Preparing a Disk for Use

Preparing the disk drive for use is a three-step process.

1. Use FDISK to insure the partitions are what you want, and in the case of original equipment manufactured (OEM) purchases, you must partition the drive. The steps needed to partition the hard drive are as follows:

   A. Create the primary DOS partition by selecting the first option, Create DOS Partition or Logical Drive, on the FDISK main menu. Then select option 1, Create Primary DOS Partition, on the submenu. Define the size you want the partition to be. Press Esc to exit.

   B. Create an extended DOS partition for any drive space that is left over by again selecting option 1 on the main menu. Then select option 2, Create Extended DOS Partition, on the submenu that appears. Define the size of the partition and the logical drive(s) you need. Press Esc to return to the main menu.

    C. Set the active partition by selecting option 2, Set the Active Partition, on the main menu and defining the active partition to be the primary DOS partition on the first hard drive. Press Esc twice to return to the DOS prompt.

2. Format the disk and place the boot-up files on the drive using the FORMAT /S command.

3. Install the operating system onto the drive. If your operating system comes on a CD-ROM, you'll have to install the CD-ROM drivers first.

Maintaining and Optimizing a Disk

Maintaining and optimizing a disk is an ongoing process. This process consists of regularly scheduled examinations of the disk drive with SCANDISK and insuring that the files on the drive are kept together as much as possible by using DEFRAG to defragment the hard drive.

SCANDISK should be run at least once a week in Standard mode to check for and repair any problems with folders, files, FAT, and lost clusters. It should also be run at least once a month in Thorough mode so that it will perform a surface scan of the hard drive. To launch SCANDISK, select Start ➤ Programs ➤ Accessories ➤ System Tools. You can also start it by typing **SCANDISK** at the DOS prompt as follows:

```
C:\SCANDISK C:
```

Fragmented hard drives are a frequently recurring problem that is caused by the way DOS saves files on the drive. As disk drives are used, files are added, deleted, and expanded on the drive. DOS fills in available disk space as it goes. This storage process forces larger files into being broken into fragments and placed in several different locations on the drive. As the drive begins to get full and fragmentation increases, system performance drops. Defragmented hard drives have all the files in contiguous clusters and don't have to work as hard jumping all over the drive as they perform their read/write operations.

DEFRAG should be run at least weekly to keep the disk drive in optimal working order. Running it daily will not cause any harm, and the utility will let you know if defragmentation is necessary at the time. DEFRAG is activated through the Start menu by selecting Programs ➤ Accessories ➤ System Tools and clicking the Defragmentation icon, or by typing **DEFRAG** at the DOS prompt as follows:

```
C:\DEFRAG
```

Exam Essentials

The following elements have a very high degree of probability of showing up on the exam.

Know the difference between FAT16 and VFAT.   FAT16 is the original FAT used by DOS. It uses a 16-bit block to store the filename, the beginning physical location of the file, its size, and the date/time it was created. It also contains additional entries for a file if the file is fragmented. VFAT is an extension of FAT16. In addition to storing the same information, VFAT has reserved areas for storing its long filenames.

Know what file allocation tables are and what they do.   File allocation tables are indexes to the data stored on the hard disk drive. They cross reference the filename with the actual location of the file on the drive. File allocation tables are used by the operating system to gain access to the files on the disk for read and write operations.

Know the different types of backups that can be performed and which ones are faster.   Backing up your data is imperative. You should not consider your computer system complete without a backup.

Be very familiar with the process of getting a new OEM hard disk drive ready for use in a PC.   First, the drive must be partitioned; then, it must be formatted; finally, it must have the operating system installed on it.

Key Terms and Concepts

Active partition: The partition that is set to hold the operating system you wish to be the default OS. For PCs, this is usually the primary DOS partition, which contains the DOS boot sector and boot files.

Archive bit: One of the flags in the file-attribute features that designates whether a file has already been backed up. When a backup occurs, the file's Archive attribute or bit is turned on to indicate it has been archived. When the file is modified, the Archive bit is turned off.

Backup: The compressed copy of the file system used to replace the file system in the event of a catastrophic failure of the hard disk drive.

Boot disk: A floppy disk with all the system files on it. When inserted into the A: drive, it will allow the system to boot. Boot disks are used to boot the system when it fails to boot off the hard disk drive.

Booting: The process of starting up the computer and loading the operating system into memory. *Cold boots* are power-on starts where the power is turned on. *Warm boots* are when you press the three-finger salute (Ctrl+Alt+Del keys) or press the restart button on the computer.

Defragmentation: The rearrangement of the files on a disk drive so that they are no longer broken up into little pieces scattered over the disk (fragmented). This process will improve system performance in any application using the hard drive.

Differential backup: The backup process that backs up all files that have not been created or changed since the last full backup, even if the file has been backed up with a differential backup before. This process does not reset the Archive bit and is not the fastest backup procedure.

Directory: The major divisions DOS uses to organize its file structure. Directories can contain files or other directories. The root directory can contain only 512 entries. If this number is exceeded, the OS will give "Disk Drive Full" messages even if the majority of the disk is empty.

Disk management: The things you have to do to keep a disk drive functioning in an optimal manner with a high degree of reliability. This includes periodic defragmentation of the drive, checks on performance, analysis of surface condition, removal or archiving of unnecessary files, and backups of the file system.

DOS boot record: An area on the disk drive that contains the DOS system files, the partition tables, and the FAT.

Extended partition: The type of DOS partition that is created after the primary DOS partition. These partitions usually contain the logical drives.

File: The actual element stored on the disk drive. Files can be broken down into three major categories. *Executable files* (.EXE, .COM, or .BAT) are files that launch programs or run commands. *System files* (.DLL, .OVL, .SYS, etc.) are used to assist other programs or system functions. *Data files* (.TXT, .DOC, .DBF, .WKS, etc.) are used by programs to store the data created by their users.

File allocation table (FAT):   A special file in the boot sector that contains information on the location of the files and directories on the disk. It acts like an index to the drive.

Full backup: The backup process that backs up every file in the file system. This process sets the Archive bit on and is the slowest backup process.

Incremental backup: The backup process that backs up only those files that have been changed since the last full or incremental backup. This process turns the Archive bit on and is the fastest backup method.

Master boot record: The portion of the boot sector that contains information about the partition.

Partitioning: The process of dividing a large hard disk drive into smaller logical spaces and assigning either logical drives or different operating systems to each partition created.

Unattended backup: A feature to look for in third-party backup utilities. It allows you to schedule a backup at a time when the system can be brought down and backed up without interfering with normal operations and productivity. When run, it is reliable enough to do so without your presence.

Virtual file allocation table (VFAT): A pseudo 32-bit FAT that allocates a reserved area within itself for the storage of long filenames. This helps the OS cross reference the long filename to FAT16 filename conventions (the 8.3 rule).

Sample Questions

1. Which method of backing up a hard disk drive is fastest?

   A. Differential

   B. Incremental

   C. Full

   D. Partial

   Answer: B. The incremental backup is the fastest since it backs up only those files modified since the last full or partial backup.

2. To prepare a disk drive for use, what are the three things, in proper order, that must be done?

   A. Format the drive, partition it, and install the operating system

   B. Install the OS, format the drive, and partition the drive

   C. Partition the drive, format it, and install the operating system

   D. Partition the drive, install the operating system, and format it

   Answer: C. Partitioning the drive sets the playing field for the drive, formatting then inserts the tracks and sectors for data mapping, and the operating system allows the system to boot from the drive. There is no other sequence in which the process can be performed.

3. How many files can a root directory of a hard disk hold?

　A. 512

　B. 1,024

　C. 2,048

　D. As many as the drive will hold

Answer: A. Due to the limitations of DOS, the root directory can have only 512 files in it. The root directory should be used only to store other directories and the necessary system files.

4. Which one of the following items contains both the short-filename and the long-filename conventions?

　A. FAT16

　B. FAT32

　C. VFAT

　D. FAT

Answer: C. Only the VFAT contains both filename conventions for backward compatibility with legacy programs.

CHAPTER

2

Memory Management

A+ Exam Objectives Covered in This Chapter:

▶ **Differentiate between types of memory.** *(pages 67 – 80)*

▶ **Identify typical memory conflict problems and how to optimize memory use.** *(pages 81 – 94)*

This objective domain requires knowledge of the types of memory used by DOS and Windows, and the potential for memory address conflicts. The major purpose of this domain is to test your knowledge of how the operating systems utilize and manage memory for various types of system and application setups. A firm grasp of this information will help you diagnose and resolve memory problems and guide you in determining the use of memory-optimization utilities.

NOTE   This material comprises 10 percent of the A+ exam. It also lends itself to the troubleshooting domain of the exam and is essential for complete understanding of the material covered in that area.

To understand the material covered in this section, you need to know the difference between memory and memory address. They are not synonymous terms. *Memory* is the physical device used to hold data and application code. This is the RAM that is installed in your system. It can been seen and touched.

Memory addresses are numeric values assigned by the CPU to locations within the physical memory and are logical in nature. They cannot be seen or touched. Memory addresses are used by the system to keep track of where it places the data and program code. CPUs have a limited number of memory addresses that they can assign to memory. The number of address lines in the CPU determines this amount. The number of address lines is determined by the architecture of the CPU. Both RAM and ROM must be assigned memory addresses for the system to recognize them. Many ROM chips, especially those in older systems, require a specific memory address.

Memory addresses are assigned to physical memory during system boot up.

Simply put, *memory management* is the techniques used to maximize the amount of conventional or base memory available for the user's programs and data. It focuses on shifting device drivers and TSRs from conventional memory into upper memory.

Differentiate between types of memory.

This objective concentrates on the different types of memory available within the computer system and how the operating system uses them. To configure your system for optimal memory use and prevent or resolve memory problems, you need to know the purpose, use, function, and location of each of the different types of memory used by the operating systems.

This section will define the following types of memory and discuss their purpose, function, and use:

- Regular DOS memory
    - Conventional, base, or low-DOS memory
    - Upper memory area, reserved memory, or high-DOS memory
- Expanded or bank-switched memory
- Extended memory
- High memory area (HMA)
- Upper memory blocks (UMBs)
- Virtual memory
- Cache memory

Critical Information

Way back in the beginning days of the PC, one of the founders of the DOS operating system is alleged to have said, "640KB of RAM is more than enough user memory." Though it took a few years to prove this wrong, we are left with the legacy of this original concept.

Those were the days of the old IBM PC/XT (with the 8088 and 8086 microprocessors), which could address a maximum of only 1 megabyte of RAM. The designers of the PC decided to allocate the memory from 640KB to 1MB for system and device BIOS functions, and let the program code, data, and other variables function within the memory below 640KB.

There are three basic reasons why there are so many different types of memory today. First, as the PC gained popularity in the business world, more and more functions were pushed off onto it—the large amounts of data involved created the need for additional memory. Second, computer programs became larger to meet the additional business demands—they stretched the 640KB limits of the XT system, creating a need for some means of addressing memory outside the normal 1-megabyte ceiling. Third, as computer architecture became capable of using memory above the 1-megabyte barrier, additional methods for addressing memory became apparent.

By knowing the material in this section, you will be able to properly configure applications, device drivers, and system variables to make the optimal use of the system's memory resources. It will also help you to understand many of the potential problems associated with memory addressing.

Regular DOS Memory

Regular DOS memory was the first memory available to DOS-based computers. Due to the architecture of the 8088 and 8086 processors, which had only a 20-bit address bus, PC/XT computers were limited to a maximum of 1 megabyte of RAM (see Figure 2.1).

F I G U R E 2.1: Regular DOS memory

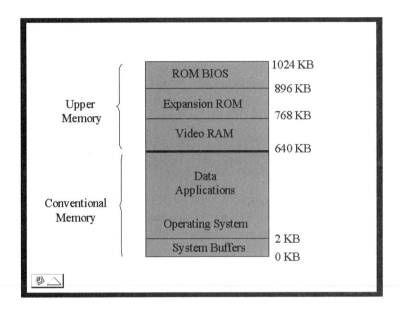

This 1MB of memory as shown in Figure 2.1 is divided into two separate areas: conventional memory and upper memory.

Conventional Memory

Conventional memory is also known as base memory or low-DOS memory. It is the portion of memory that starts at zero bytes in RAM and goes to the 640KB mark in RAM. As Figure 2.1 illustrates, conventional memory is used to:

- Load and run active applications

- Load and process data currently needed by the active programs

- Hold and run the operating system (18KB to 90KB of memory are needed to run DOS, depending on the version you are using)

- Keep a reserved area (zero to 2KB) for system requirements

All program operations in a DOS-based computer system take place within the conventional memory area. Your programs, the data they need for processing, the results of the processing, all program variables, and the operating system run within conventional memory.

Modern applications are memory hungry and require an enormous portion of memory. Coupled with the amount of memory needed for the operating system and other system requirements, there is little room left for data. This demand for memory resources has created a situation that has become known as *RAM cram*, which occurs when too many demands are placed on available memory resources. RAM cram can be the source of all sorts of system problems.

RAM cram is caused by the 640KB barrier. This DOS barrier is the limitation DOS placed on the amount of memory available for programmers to use for their applications. Placing the reserved (or upper) memory area on top of the memory pool created a steel wall beyond which programs could not run.

Upper Memory

Upper memory is also known as reserved memory and high-DOS memory. The reserved block of memory (from 640KB to 1MB) is set aside for video RAM, system ROM BIOS, and expansion card ROM such as video cards and controller cards.

Figure 2.1 shows this 384KB memory area configured as follows:

- 640KB to 768KB is used for video RAM memory. Areas are assigned for monochrome, CGA, EGA, and VGA displays.

- 768KB to 896KB is reserved for installable ROMs such as video cards and controller cards.

- 896KB to 1,024KB (1MB) is reserved for system ROM BIOS.

The upper memory is not fully populated. Unused blocks of memory exist within this area. If you are using a color monitor, the monochrome area could be free. Additionally, some of the blocks of memory set aside for expansion-card ROM will be available if you have not used them all.

Expanded Memory

The availability of sections of reserved memory led to the development of *expanded memory*. Since the early PC/XT computers could not address memory beyond the 1MB limit, a method was needed to add memory to the system while making it seem like there was still only 1MB with which to work. A solution was found in bank switching additional areas of memory into and out of the reserved memory as page frames. This solution called for a combination of hardware and software components.

The hardware was a specially designed expansion board containing as much as 32MB of RAM that exists apart from and outside of the system's main 1MB memory. Figure 2.2 illustrates the basic concepts involved in using expanded memory.

FIGURE 2.2: Expanded memory

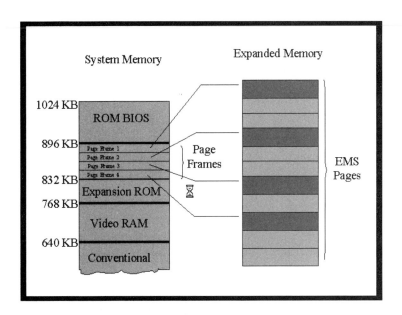

The software, in the form of a device manager, divided the available reserved memory areas into four 16KB blocks called *page frames*.

These page frames acted as windows into the expanded memory area. These windows could be used to shuttle data back and forth between the system's main memory and the expanded memory board. The data used in expanded memory were copied back and forth between the page frame and the expanded memory page.

Since the page frame exists within the 1MB range of the system's memory address limit, applications could map these page frames to memory addresses on the expanded memory board. The system, in combination with the expanded memory device and its driver, is able to address up to 32MB of RAM while seeing only 1MB to address.

To use this technology, applications had to be developed to take advantage of it, and hardware had to be designed to a specific standard that would allow the applications to operate reliably. Lotus, Intel, and Microsoft developed a standard called the LIM standard for expanded memory management. The latest version, LIM 4, moves both data and applications into expanded memory as needed.

Extended Memory

Extended memory is any memory above 1,024KB (see Figure 2.3). Extended memory can be addressed on only 286 and later machines. The 80286 and 80386 microprocessors can address up to 16MB of memory. The 486 and Pentium microprocessors have varying limits due to motherboard configurations, but are able to address up to 4GB of physical memory; the Pentium can address as much as 1TB of virtual memory. All memory above the 1MB level is extended memory.

DOS is closely linked to the 8088 and 8086 microprocessors and can work with only the first 1MB of memory. Since extended memory is beyond this range, DOS cannot normally run programs in extended memory, but can use it for RAMDISK drives, disk caches, print buffers, and other data-storage needs. DOS can also load itself into the first 64KB of extended memory, which is called the high memory area (HMA), and it can simulate expanded memory for those applications that need it. Applications, if so designed, can page blocks of program code into and out of extended memory.

F I G U R E 2.3: Extended memory

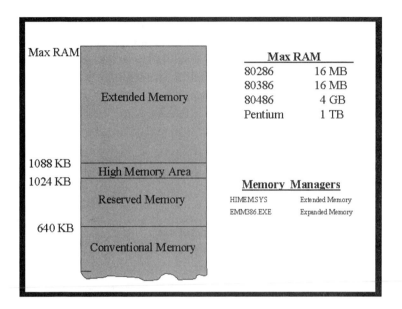

For DOS to run programs in extended memory, the programs must be extended-DOS applications. These programs switch the microprocessor from Real mode into Protected mode. Once the application has finished, the microprocessor is switched back into Real mode. This is the method Windows 3.*x* uses to get DOS to perform its multi-tasking processes.

For DOS to use extended memory, it has to have an extended memory manager such as HIMEM.SYS loaded through the CONFIG.SYS file during boot up. HIMEM.SYS takes charge of all extended memory and insures that it is available for XMS-compatible applications running on an 80286 or better microprocessor. It also works at preventing system errors due to memory conflicts. HIMEM.SYS gains access to extended memory through the A20 handler, an address line on 80286 and later microprocessors that provides a direct channel into extended memory.

High Memory Area (HMA)

High memory area (HMA) is the first 64KB of extended memory (see Figure 2.3). The HMA is an unusual phenomenon. Any attempt on an 8088 machine at addressing memory above the 1MB ceiling causes the microprocessor to wrap around to memory address zero. Starting with the 80286, microprocessors can map this 64KB area between the 1,024KB ceiling and the beginning of memory into the HMA. Once HIMEM.SYS is loaded, DOS can directly access the HMA without going into Protected mode.

The most common use for the HMA is to load the majority of DOS into it. This frees up approximately 50KB of conventional memory. Only one utility, application, or TSR can occupy the HMA at any one time, regardless of its size.

Upper Memory Blocks (UMBs)

Upper memory blocks (UMBs) are located in the reserved memory area. They are unused portions of memory between the 768KB to 960KB range. Since user memory actually stops at 640KB, these areas cannot be used to run a program—there is no RAM there. These areas are meant to be filled in by on-board ROM from expansion cards.

By creating UMBs, portions of extended memory can be mapped into these available areas of upper memory. Once they are created, you can load device drivers and Terminate and Stay Resident (TSR) programs into them. This frees up additional RAM in your conventional memory area for those super memory hogs. UMBs are created with the DOS=UMB command in CONFIG.SYS.

Virtual Memory

Virtual memory is the method of simulating RAM by using a portion of the hard disk drive. The space on the disk drive acts as part of the system's total available memory. The contents of a part of memory are spooled onto the hard disk drive to free up RAM for immediate use. The data placed on the hard disk drive are then called back into RAM as needed, and another portion of data is spooled off onto the disk drive. This technique allows the computer to use more memory than is actually installed on the machine.

This method of memory management is very slow due to the mechanical movements required by the hard disk drive. It can also be very disk intensive and can cause disk thrashing, which places undue stress on the hard disk drive and leads to premature failure of the disk drive.

Windows makes extensive use of virtual memory by using a *swap file*—data that are not currently needed are spooled (or swapped) onto the disk drive and reloaded when needed.

Memory Cache

Memory cache or cache memory is a small amount of fast static RAM (usually around 64KB for older machines and 512KB for newer machines) used to store data recently accessed from the disk drive that the microprocessor may need again. Storing data in this manner relieves the processor from having to relocate them on the disk drive, giving an additional boost to system performance.

Exam Essentials

Memory is an essential part of understanding how a computer operating system functions. To optimize your system or resolve problems with it, you must have first-hand knowledge of the different types and functions of memory as well as the terminology used to describe them.

Know the basic types and purposes of memory used within PCs. From the operating system's viewpoint, there are four basic types of RAM: conventional memory, upper memory area, expanded memory, and extended memory.

Be familiar with the breakdown of the memory tree. Conventional memory: zero to 640KB; upper memory: 640KB to 1MB; video RAM: 640KB to 768KB; expansion ROM: 768KB to 896KB; system ROM BIOS: 896KB to 1,024KB; and extended memory: over 1,024KB.

Be familiar with the way DOS can use high memory areas with extended memory. Usually there are blocks of memory addresses within the expansion ROM area (768KB to 896KB) that are not used. These memory ranges do not have RAM assigned to them since they were designed as a place to map ROM memory addresses for expansion devices that needed them. These empty blocks can be recovered by the operating system by mapping portions of extended memory to them. This process is accomplished with the DOS=UMB command in CONFIG.SYS, which creates upper memory blocks that are mapped to the available areas of upper memory.

Know the concepts involved in virtual memory. Virtual memory is a combination of system RAM and a portion of the hard disk space. The overall effect is to increase the amount of total RAM beyond what is actually installed in the system. Portions of RAM are transferred back and forth from memory to the disk drive as needed.

Know the difference between extended and expanded memory. *Extended* memory is memory that can be addressed by the operating system in a linear fashion (e.g., from 1MB to 4GB). It is an extension of the main memory used by the operating system. Extended memory requires the use of an extended memory manager such as HIMEM.SYS. *Expanded* memory is outside the normal linear addressing scheme. It is paged into and out of designated areas in the upper memory range. Expanded memory requires the use of an expanded memory manager such as EMM386.EXE.

Key Terms and Concepts

Address: A location in memory. Each byte of memory has a specific place within the memory tree where it resides. Addresses are used to place and find elements of a program, data, or variable. Everything used in the computer has an address associated with it.

AT computer: A computer based on the 80286 or later microprocessor that can address more than 1MB of memory.

Backfill: The method of mapping expanded memory into conventional memory to bring the total amount of conventional memory up to the 640KB limit.

Bank switching: A dynamic process that allows the data from an expanded memory card to be transferred back and forth between regular system memory and expanded memory.

BIOS (Basic Input/Output System): A ROM-based software that acts as an interpreter between the operating system and the hardware it represents.

Contiguous memory: Memory occurring in a single, continuous block.

Conventional memory: The lower 640KB of RAM in which DOS and applications run, and data are stored and manipulated.

Device driver: A small program designed to facilitate communication between a device and the computer system. Using the proper device driver will yield the most optimal performance of the device.

Disk cache: A small amount of high-speed memory used to store data read from the hard disk drive. If the system needs the information again, it looks in the cache—if it is still there, the system loads it from the cache instead of from the disk drive. This causes a considerable boost in access performance.

DRAM (dynamic random access memory): This type of memory is used extensively within computer systems since it is cheaper to manufacture. DRAM requires the contents of memory to be periodically refreshed by the operating system to retain the data in it.

EMM386.SYS: Reserved memory manager that emulates expanded memory in the extended memory area and gives DOS the ability to utilize upper memory blocks.

Expanded memory (EMS): Memory that is outside the normal address range of the computer system. This memory (up to 32MB) can be accessed with the use of an expanded memory manager, which allows data to be paged (or bank switched) between the expanded memory and page frames located in the upper memory area.

Extended memory (XMS): Memory above the 1MB ceiling on 80286 and above microprocessors. Extended memory can be accessed only while the CPU is in Protected mode.

Gigabyte (GB): Approximately one billion bytes.

High memory area (HMA): The first 64KB of extended memory found on 80286 and later microprocessors.

High-DOS memory: Another name for upper or reserved memory.

HIMEM.SYS: The extended memory manager that enables DOS to use memory above the 1MB limit.

Kilobyte (KB): Approximately 1,000 bytes (actually, it is 1,024 bytes).

Low-DOS memory: Another name for conventional memory.

MEM.EXE: The DOS command that allows you to examine how much memory you have and how it is being used. To see how memory is being used, you must use the /C switch.

Motherboard memory: Memory that can be directly inserted into the motherboard.

Page: A 16KB block of expanded memory. The size of the bank switched in and out of regular memory.

Page frame: A 64KB block of upper memory used to hold an EMS page. Four page frames are created in upper memory when an expanded memory manager is activated. Four EMS pages can be mapped to these four page frames on a one-to-one basis.

Protected mode: The mode of an AT-based computer that allows memory addressing beyond the 1MB limit. It also assigns memory ranges for applications and then protects them from being over-written by other applications.

RAM (random access memory): The contents in RAM are changeable and volatile. If power goes off, the contents of RAM cease to exist.

RAM disk: An area of memory that has been set aside to act as a regular hard disk drive. It is assigned a drive letter and can be used exactly like a hard drive, with one exception—saving data to the RAM drive is not permanent storage. The contents of the RAM drive must be copied onto the hard drive before the system is turned off. Since RAM drives are much faster than hard drives, they make an excellent place to store the temporary files created by Windows.

Real mode: The basic mode of XT-based systems. This is DOS's native mode. On AT-based machines, the Real mode makes the system perform like a super-fast XT.

Reserved memory: Another name for the upper or high-DOS memory area.

ROM (read only memory):   Memory that contains program code or data that are needed by the system. The contents are installed at the factory and cannot be changed.

Shadow RAM: The RAM that contains a copy of ROM and is mapped to the ROM address. See *Shadow ROM*.

Shadow ROM: The process of copying the contents of a ROM BIOS into a RAM location and then mapping the ROM address to this RAM address. Since RAM is faster than ROM, this usually speeds up the system.

SIMM (single in-line memory module):   A type of RAM used in more modern computers. It consists of a bank of RAM chips installed on a specially designed expansion card.

SRAM (static random access memory):   This type of RAM can be written to once and does not need periodic refreshing. It is a more expensive type of memory and is much faster than DRAM.

TSR (Terminate and Stay Resident):   A small program that, once activated, resides in the background and is not normally seen during the operation of the system. TSRs are normally placed in UMBs. A prime example of a TSR is an antivirus program that guards your system against possible virus attacks while you load things off a floppy diskette or download from the Internet.

UMBs (upper memory blocks): Areas in upper memory that are not utilized by video RAM, system BIOS, or device ROMs. Expanded memory managers can map extended memory to these blocks if the DOS=UMB command has been used in CONFIG.SYS.

Video memory: The part of upper memory that stores the image of the computer's display.

Virtual memory: A combination of physical RAM and hard disk storage put aside for use as memory. The OS swaps portions out of memory onto the hard drive and back again as needed.

XT computer: The original design of the IBM PC and compatibles. It includes the 8088 and 8086 microprocessors. These computers can address a maximum of 1MB and operate in the Real mode.

Sample Questions

1. What is the UMA?

   A. The area of memory between 640KB and 1MB

   B. The memory that allows the use of EMS pages

   C. The first 16MB of extended memory

   D. The first 64KB of extended memory

   Answer: D. The upper memory area is the first 64KB of extended memory.

2. What does HIMEM.SYS have to do with virtual memory?

   A. It sets up the memory to accept DOS.

   B. It sets up the memory to accept pages of data.

   C. It sets up the disk drive to act as part of RAM.

   D. It has nothing to do with it.

   Answer: D. HIMEM.SYS is the extended memory manager and sets up the operating system to use extended memory, not virtual memory.

Identify typical memory conflict problems and how to optimize memory use.

This objective focuses on the various types of problems that can be caused by the system's memory and the generally recognized steps used to prevent and fix them. The following topics will be addressed:

- Memory conflicts
- Illegal operations
- Windows 95 and 16-bit application conflicts
- Memory-optimization utilities
- Gaining access to upper memory with HIMEM.SYS
- Expanded memory blocks

Critical Information

With the ever-increasing demand placed on system resources by applications and data, it is no wonder that problems occur. What is really a wonder is that they don't happen much more frequently. To understand the problems associated with memory conflicts and how they occur, you need to learn how the operating systems manage memory.

Memory Management

Memory management is one of the most critical tasks assigned to an operating system. DOS, Windows 3.*x*, and Windows 95 have their own ways of handling memory. If you know the basic processes they use, it will help you understand what can go wrong.

DOS

DOS is a 16-bit operating system and is limited to a maximum memory address of 1MB. The goal of memory management under DOS is to boost as many device drivers, OS components, and TSRs into UMB and extended memory as possible.

DOS uses HIMEM.SYS and EMM386.EXE to accomplish this task. Both are loaded into the system through CONFIG.SYS.

- *HIMEM.SYS* is a device driver for memory above the 1MB level. It allows DOS to access the first bank (or 64KB) of this area of memory.

- *EMM386.EXE* is a device driver that manages expanded memory. It also allows TSRs and other devices to be loaded into the upper memory area—to do so, the DOS=UMB line must be in the CONFIG.SYS file. For EMM386.EXE to work, HIMEM.SYS must be loaded first.

Another command line used in CONFIG.SYS is DOS=HIGH, UMB. This command loads a major portion of DOS into the high memory area (HMA) and creates upper memory blocks (UMBs) in the upper memory area.

The DEVICEHIGH = *device name* command is used in CONFIG.SYS to load device drivers into the UMBs. The LOADHIGH or LH command is used in AUTOEXEC.BAT to load TSRs into the UMBs.

To check memory usage, you can use the MEM /C command, which will display the total amount of memory, the amount of memory still available, and the device drivers and TSRs that are occupying memory.

To optimize memory usage, you can either manually edit the CONFIG.SYS and AUTOEXEC.BAT files and insert the proper commands to load the device drivers and TSRs as needed, or make the MEMMAKER command do it for you. Optimizing memory manually is a long, tedious process that involves determining how much upper memory is available and then trying to assign the combination of device drivers and TSRs that will free up the most conventional memory.

Using the MEMMAKER command to optimize memory is the fastest and easiest method. All the hard work is done for you. At a minimum, you must have the following major commands in CONFIG.SYS:

- DEVICE=HIGHMEM.SYS

- DEVICE=EMM386.EXE

- DOS=HIGH,UMB

These files make it possible for DOS to see the upper and extended memory, use upper memory blocks, and load itself into high memory area.

NOTE Using MEMMAKER does have some risks. It is not an intelligent agent. You must check the CONFIG.SYS file to ensure that it has inserted all the major commands in the right place and order.

Windows 3.x

Since Windows 3.x is only a GUI that resides on top of DOS, DOS performs the majority of Windows 3.x's memory-management tasks. Windows 3.x throws a few extra components into the memory-management mix:

- Temporary files

- Virtual memory

Temporary files are created as needed by Windows and its applications. These files contain data and variable settings needed by the program or the OS for future reference. These files are usually deleted by the program that created it when they are no longer needed. If not, Windows deletes them during a proper shutdown procedure. These temporary files are located in the directory specified by the TEMP variable in AUTOEXEC.BAT, as in the following example:

```
SET TEMP=C:\WINDOWS\TEMP
```

For some reason, DOS 6 uses the following command to set the TEMP variable:

SET TEMP=C:\DOS

Sharing a major directory of important and permanent files with a bunch of temporary files is not a good idea. You should check your AUTOEXEC.BAT file and change the TEMP variable to another directory, such as

SET TEMP=C:\TEMP

Then, make sure you have created the TEMP directory.

Virtual memory is available to Windows 3.*x* only while it is in Enhanced mode. This means you must use a 80386 or later computer to take advantage of virtual memory. Virtual memory extensively uses swap files that it switches back and forth between memory and allocated space on the hard disk drive. Windows can provide virtual memory in two ways:

Temporary swap file: The temporary swap file creates and uses a file called WIN386.SWP.

Permanent swap file: The permanent swap file creates and uses a file called 386SPART.PAR.

The *temporary swap file* is a dynamic file that changes its size under Windows 3.*x*'s direction and according to the needs of the moment. Temporary swap files can become fragmented and slow the performance of the whole system. In addition, because the size of the swap file must be constantly adjusted to meet current needs, it also leads to slower operations.

The *permanent swap file* is a designated static-sized file. When a permanent swap file is initiated, a portion of contiguous clusters on the hard drive is assigned as the swap file. Since it cannot be fragmented and does not have to undergo resizing, the permanent swap file is the faster of the two.

You can change swap-file parameters using the Windows Control Panel by selecting Virtual Memory from the 386 Enhanced Program option.

Windows 95

For all the hype to the contrary, Windows 95 is just a super combination of DOS and Windows 3.11 with a few extra features thrown in. Memory configuration is still the same as with DOS, but Windows 95 has some significant improvements in the way it allocates memory addresses and in its automated memory optimization.

Windows 95 incorporates a few new features that enable it to perform its preemptive multi-tasking functions and work with DOS-based programs in this multi-tasking environment. These new features are as follows:

- Virtual machine manager
- Virtual device drivers
- Memory heaps

The *virtual machine manager* is the processes that control the virtual machines Windows sets up to meet the needs of each type of application that it runs. A *virtual machine* is a pseudo machine that is set up in an area of the computer's memory. The application that is running in it thinks that it is running in a DOS-like environment all by itself. To create a virtual machine, Windows 95 sets aside a block of memory for the application and copies the first 1MB of memory addresses into it. Windows 95 places every application it runs into one of these virtual machines.

The virtual machine manager monitors these virtual machines, determines what resources they need, and controls when they can have access to them. This usually allows DOS-based programs to operate effectively and efficiently within their own environments without getting in the way of other programs and causing problems such as hangups, reboots, and GPFs. The virtual machines give Windows 95 its preemptive multi-tasking capability. If a program crashes, it dies within its own environment and, theoretically, does not cause any problems within the overall system.

The *virtual device drivers* (VDDs or VxDs) are 32-bit device drivers running in Protected mode used by Windows 95 to interface with hardware devices attached to the system. These VxDs emulate the 16-bit DOS-based device drivers and act as sentinels between the DOS-based applications and the devices. DOS programs are designed to be the only active application on the system. As such, they want to hog all the devices they need. In a multi-tasking environment, this can cause some serious problems. The VxDs prevent DOS programs from hogging the system devices by intercepting the DOS requests for service and allowing access to the device only when it is appropriate for the application.

An example is the keyboard. DOS expects to have complete and unlimited access to the keyboard. As far as DOS is concerned, anything entered at the keyboard is for DOS to deal with. The VxDs intercept such demands and give access only to the keyboard when the keyboard entries are for that particular DOS-based application.

Memory heaps are memory areas set aside for programs and their data. When a program is loaded, the OS assigns part of the heap to it. When the program terminates and is unloaded from memory, it frees the memory assigned to it for reallocation to other programs. Windows 95 organizes its memory into five heaps and allocates portions of memory from each heap to every application that is loaded. The heaps are as follows:

GDI heap: Memory used for the graphics display such as icons, pointer, fonts, and backgrounds

Menu heap: Memory used to contain menus and their options

System heap: Memory that the OS assigns to programs and their virtual machines

Text heap: Memory that holds the text used by Windows

User heap: Memory that holds the data for the desktop and user interface

Windows 95 also has 32-bit Protected-mode drivers that are loaded automatically into extended memory. This process virtually eliminates the need for CONFIG.SYS unless you are running DOS-based programs. These device drivers allow the OS to assign a set of memory address blocks to an application, then contain the application within that range of memory. This method of allocating memory prevents one application from overstepping its boundaries and overwriting another program's memory area. Of course, these drivers work effectively only with 32-bit applications, which have additional control features built into them. Older Windows 3.*x* and DOS programs are not as easily controlled.

Windows also loads the virtual memory managers automatically. By default, the swap file is a dynamic file that changes size with system needs. Due to the 32-bit disk-access method that Windows 95 uses, making the swap file a permanent swap file gains very little in system performance.

The technological design of Windows 95 provides two basic rings or levels of protection for system and application files. The virtual machine manager and the virtual device drivers share the highest level of protection in the inner ring, while everything else resides in the outer ring. This includes the system kernel, the graphical device interface (GDI), the user interface, and both Win32 and Win16 programs.

The KERNEL-32, GDI-32, and USER-32 files are the system files designed for the Windows 95 environment. Applications that are designed for Windows 95 are also 32-bit–based applications. Windows 95 copies these system files into the virtual machines that it creates for these 32-bit applications. When one of these programs crashes, it does not corrupt or lock up the entire system. Due to the extra control features built into 32-bit programs and system files, they simply die quietly within their own virtual-machine environment and are tidied up by the OS.

For backward compatibility, Microsoft inserted a separate set of system files for DOS-based programs. These are the KERNEL-16, GDI-16, and USER-16 files. These files are copied into the virtual machines that are created to support DOS and Windows 3.*x* programs. When one of these programs crashes, it can take out the entire system.

Problems Associated with Memory

Many times, the operating system is not up to the task of managing memory, so conflicts over memory arise. Most computer problems can be traced back to memory conflicts caused by programs that have tried to use memory allocated to another program or have not released the memory allocated to them when they are terminated.

Memory Conflicts

Memory conflicts are problems that occur when two programs try to use the same memory address at the same time. In most cases, the problem can be tracked down to a DOS/Windows 3.*x* application. The 16-bit programs do not have the extra control features built into them that prevent them from taking full advantage of Protected mode. When memory gets low, these applications and utilities will take what they need even at the expense of another program. Memory conflicts can also be caused by corrupted program files or device drivers that cause erroneous readings by the OS, which then assigns them the wrong resources.

You can suspect a memory conflict when your system locks up, you get a GPF, or the system displays an illegal-operation error message. Memory conflicts are not the only things that cause these errors. However, if you have less than 16MB of memory, are running DOS/Windows 3.*x* programs or TSRs, and/or the system is operating with only 20 percent of resources available, a memory conflict is a definite possibility. Possible solutions include increasing the amount of RAM and replacing the DOS/Windows 3.*x* programs with Windows 95 versions.

Memory Leaks

A *memory leak* is a problem in which an application (16- or 32-bit) does not release its assigned memory addresses when it terminates and is unloaded from the system. This reduces the amount of memory the memory heaps have available for allocation to new programs.

The most common symptom for this problem is out-of-memory errors. The GDI and system heaps are the heaps that will, in most cases, be used to the maximum and be pushed to maximum fill. If memory is not released by terminating applications, these heaps soon run out of memory. The only solution to this problem is to turn your computer off and turn it back on. This clears all heaps and resets them to the maximum memory available.

Errors Associated with Memory Problems

Error messages are ambiguous entities. They say one thing, but what they indicate may not be anything close to the problem that generated the error message. Too many things can go wrong within a modern computer system—writing separate messages for all of them, even if all of them could be determined, would take up too much ROM. So, programmers compromised on preciseness in favor of keeping the amount of memory occupied by these messages to a minimum. Every error message pulls multiple duty, especially those associated with memory.

The basic error messages associated with memory are as follows:

Illegal Operations: When associated with memory, this error message usually means that a 16-bit program has stepped on some other program or a system memory space. It can also mean that you have two device drivers occupying the same memory address.

Out of Memory: This error can mean you have reached the limits of your physical memory, but in most cases it means that one or more heaps have run dry of available memory due to a memory leak.

General Protection Fault: Once again, a misbehaved 16-bit program that has tried to take some territory from another application usually causes this error.

Windows 95 and 16-Bit Application Conflicts

Windows 95 is basically a 32-bit operating system, while DOS is a 16-bit operating system. To provide backward compatibility for Windows 95, Microsoft designed a lot of 16-bit operations into the OS.

These 16-bit operations share the same protection level (ring) as the 32-bit operations. To make matters worse, both are in the same ring as the OS kernel. An errant application can wreak havoc with the OS kernel. Since the 32-bit programs have additional control features built into them, they do not cause a problem. The 16-bit applications can and do cause problems.

In addition, the first 1MB of memory that is copied into each virtual machine is a two-way street. Changes to system variables made within any of the virtual machines can be passed back into the real 1MB area and affect the OS itself. Again, the 32-bit programs are more isolated from each other due to the additional control features, but 16-bit applications can and do make indiscriminant changes.

DOS-based programs by their very nature are self-centered, selfish hogs. They expect to get everything all of the time. They do not know how to share. Coupled with their limited self control, these applications often overpower the OS with their incessant demands and hoggish appetites. The result is system lockups, GPFs, and illegal operations.

If you want to prevent these conflicts, you will have to upgrade all of your 16-bit applications and utilities, from that neat little screen saver and antivirus program to the full-blown applications to which you have become attached. They should be replaced by programs specially written for Windows 95 and that are 32-bit–based programs. If replacement is not an option, you can contact the companies that have written your 16-bit programs and try installing the latest drivers they have for them. If your system has less than 16MB of memory, upgrade it to 16MB or more.

Memory-Optimization Utilities

MEMMAKER is the memory-optimization utility that comes with the OS. It is used with DOS/Windows 3.*x* to gain maximum amounts of conventional memory with the least effort. It reads your CONFIG.SYS and AUTOEXEC.BAT files to see which drivers and utilities you need to load, and then performs some high-speed calculations on where to best place each of the drivers and utilities. After it has determined where to place each of the components, it modifies CONFIG.SYS and AUTOEXEC.BAT to reflect the decisions it has made.

To ensure that MEMMAKER works successfully, you need to verify that your CONFIG.SYS file is set up to do the following things:

- Gain access to upper memory: HIMEM.SYS

- Use expanded memory blocks: EMM386.EXE

- Set up UMBs: DOS=UMB

- Load DOS into the HMA: DOS=HIGH

The following CONFIG.SYS is the basic commands you need to have before you run MEMMAKER:

```
REM Basic Entries to Config.Sys
device=c:\dos\himem.sys
device=c:\dos\emm386.exe
dos=high,umb
files=40
REM Enter the rest of your device drivers and setups
here
```

With the above entries, MEMMAKER should be able to free up some of the conventional memory. To be certain, check the results and verify that as many of your drivers and TSRs have been loaded into UMBs. It is usually a good idea to use MEM /C before and after using MEMMAKER just to see how effective it was.

Exam Essentials

To prepare for this exam objective, you need to fully understand what can go wrong with the system memory and be very familiar with the utilities used in CONFIG.SYS and AUTOEXEC.BAT that have an impact on memory optimization.

Know the different types of memory problems, what causes them, and what can be done to overcome them.   Memory conflicts are problems that occur when one application tries to use a memory address allocated to another program. The most common causes are misbehaved 16-bit programs or a severe shortage of available memory. The solution to this problem is to increase the amount of RAM you have in the system and replace the 16-bit programs with 32-bit Windows 95 programs.

Memory leaks are problems caused when an application fails to surrender its allocated memory addresses when it exits the system. To solve this problem, you need to perform a cold boot to reset the memory heaps. Getting the latest patches for the program may also help.

Know what is involved in a Windows 95 conflict with a 16-bit application. Windows is a 32-bit OS. A 16-bit application works within the 32-bit environment, but does not have the control features needed to make it totally compliant with the OS. A conflict occurs when the application tries to perform an operation outside the parameters assigned to it by the OS. This can result in an illegal-operation error or a complete system lockup. Possible solutions to this problem are replacing the 16-bit application with a 32-bit version or getting the latest version updates.

Know how to set up a system for optimal memory utilization. Memory optimization starts with the CONFIG.SYS file. You must have HIMEM.SYS, EMM386.EXE, and DOS=HIGH,UMB command lines to configure the system for accessing upper and extended memory. DEVICEHIGH commands are then used in CONFIG.SYS to load device drivers into these locations, and LOADHIGH command lines are used in AUTOEXEC.BAT to load TSRs into these areas.

Key Terms and Concepts

Application Program Interface (API):   A set of rules that determines what a program can and cannot do within the system.

EMM386.EXE: A DOS utility used to manage upper memory blocks.

Enhanced mode: The operational mode of a microprocessor (80386 and later) that allows it to access extended memory and perform multi-tasking.

General Protection Fault (GPF): An error message that occurs when Windows tries to use a memory address that is no longer available to it.

Heap: A block of memory set aside for programs and data.

HIMEM.SYS: A DOS utility that allows DOS to use memory above the 1MB range.

Illegal-Operation error: An error message telling you that the named application has tried to do something outside the parameters dictated by the API or that the application has tried to access memory addresses that were not within its virtual-machine boundaries.

MEM command: A DOS utility that displays the way memory is being used by the system.

MEMMAKER command: A DOS utility that automatically determines the best methods to use for optimizing memory. It modifies CONFIG.SYS and AUTOEXEC.BAT to reflect the results of its analysis.

Memory conflict: A problem caused by two programs that try to use the same memory address.

Memory leak: A problem caused by an application that fails to release its allocated memory before it exits the system.

Memory management: The process of optimizing memory resources by freeing up as much conventional memory as possible.

Memory mapping: The process of assigning memory addresses to physical memory for both ROM and RAM. It occurs during boot up.

MSD: A DOS utility used to view system information. Can be used to check memory allocations for including and excluding UMBs with the EMM386.EXE utility.

Real mode: The mode of the original microprocessor (8088 and 8086) that allowed it to address up to 1MB of memory.

Sample Questions

1. What is a memory conflict?

   A. A problem in which one application tries to take memory allocated to another program

   B. A problem in which an application fails to return allocated memory when it exits the system

   C. A problem in which two files try to load into the computer at the same time

   D. A problem in which one memory heap overwrites another one

   Answer: A. A memory conflict occurs when a program tries to use memory that has been allocated to another program.

2. Which of the following utilities is used to create upper memory blocks?

   A. HIMEM.SYS

   B. EMM386.EXE

   C. DOS=HIGH,UMB

   D. MEM /C

   Answer: C. HIMEM.SYS makes upper memory available, EMM386.EXE manages and places items into the UMBs, and DOS=UMB creates the UMBs.

CHAPTER

3

Installation, Configuration,
and Upgrading

A+ Exam Objectives Covered in This Chapter:

▶ Identify the procedures for installing DOS, Windows 3.*x*, and Windows 95, and for bringing the software to a basic operational level. *(pages 97 – 122)*

▶ Identify steps to perform an operating system upgrade. *(pages 122 – 128)*

▶ Identify the basic system boot sequences and alternative ways to boot the system software, including the steps to create an emergency boot disk with utilities installed. *(pages 128 – 139)*

▶ Identify procedures for loading/adding device drivers and the necessary software for certain devices. *(pages 139 – 151)*

▶ Identify the procedures for changing options, configuring, and using the Windows printing subsystem. *(pages 152 – 158)*

▶ Identify the procedures for installing and launching typical Windows and non-Windows applications. *(pages 159 – 164)*

The major purpose of this domain of the examination is to test your knowledge of what is involved in the installation, configuration, and upgrading of the operating systems, software components, and major hardware components of the operating system.

A firm grasp of these objectives will eliminate a lot of the hassle from the installation and upgrading process, and allow you to easily add new software and hardware components to your system.

NOTE   This material comprises 25 percent of the exam. Installation may seem like a mundane subject that is fully automated by most modern setup routines, but it does take up a significant portion of the exam. The exam also hits on many of the finer details of installation and configuration. You need to spend some time mastering these objectives to be fully prepared for this portion of the exam.

Identify the procedures for installing DOS, Windows 3.*x*, and Windows 95, and for bringing the software to a basic operational level.

The objective for this section focuses on the process of getting a hard disk drive ready for operation. To be prepared for this section of the exam, you will have know how to use FDISK, FORMAT, and SETUP.

You will also have to be familiar with the command lines normally found in CONFIG.SYS and AUTOEXEC.BAT.

Critical Information

The preparation of your hard disk drive and the installation of the operating system are the genesis of your system. The amount of time you spend on planning how you will partition your drive to best suit your current and future needs will save you an enormous amount of future frustration. In the same vein, the amount of time you spend on the meticulous installation and configuration of your operating system will also pay off in the long run.

Most users approach the installation process as a major annoyance that has to be put up with to get to the fun stuff. However, the operating system is the foundation of your entire system. The wise builder always insures that their structures are built on firm foundations and that the ground under the foundations is as sound as solid rock. They know that proper planning and preparation are essential to success, and that the added time spent on the smallest details and doing things right the first time is worth it compared to the time spent trying to fix things after the fact.

NOTE Failure to plan is planning to fail. Proper planning and extra effort in preparing the hard drive will save you tons of frustration and aggravation. If you load your OS and applications then find out you need another partition, it can be a real headache.

Just like a building cannot be constructed without the foundation, a disk drive cannot be used by the system until the drive has been partitioned and formatted. The OS does not recognize an unpartitioned drive. When you try to access an unpartitioned drive, it will result in a drive-not-present error message, even with the drive properly hooked up. You will not be able to change to the drive. Once the drive has been partitioned, you will be able to CD to the drive. If you try to access any information on an unformatted disk drive, it will give you a read error message.

With this in mind, the critical procedures needed to set up a computer system and get it running at its basic operational level will be explored.

Partitioning a Hard Disk Drive

Partitioning a hard drive involves creating the partition(s) you need on the drive. It produces a file in the boot sector of the drive called the partition table. The *partition table* contains all the information concerning the number of partitions you have divided the drive into, the starting and ending sector for each partition, and the type of partition you have set each partition to be. It also contains the information about the logical drives assigned to each partition if you have done so.

Hard disk drives can be purchased formatted or unformatted. In most cases, the hard disk drive that comes with a new computer system will already be partitioned and formatted, and have the operating system installed on it. For the most part, disk drives you purchase separately, especially OEM drives, will need to be partitioned and formatted before they are used.

To partition a disk drive, you use the DOS utility FDISK. To partition a hard drive, you boot from a bootable floppy disk that contains the operating system files, and FDISK and FORMAT commands. Once the system has been booted, FDISK is entered at the command prompt—the utility takes over and will display a menu with four options on it. Please refer to the "Necessary Procedures" section for more details.

If you will run DOS or Windows 95, you must install the operating system in the primary drive's active partition.

NOTE   The primary drive is the first drive (e.g.,C:). The active partition is the partition that is read at start-up. The active directory is set using the appropriate menu option in FDISK.

If you have divided the drive into several partitions, you must also assign logical disk drives to each of the DOS or Windows 95 partitions.

Formatting a Hard Disk Drive

When you format a drive electronically, it places the tracks and sectors on the disk drive and creates the file allocation table (FAT). Every partition to which you have assigned a logical partition must be formatted individually.

The active partition on the primary drive must have the operating system files installed on it. The external commands may be located on another logical drive or a separate physical drive.

The FORMAT /S command is used to format the primary disk's active partition. This command will also copy the system files onto the partition. The system files can be installed only on the active partition. All other hard drives (logical or physical) do not require the /S switch.

Installing the Operating System

After partitioning and formatting the hard drive, you will need to install an operating system and set up a user environment before the drive is ready for use. For DOS-based machines, you would install

DOS for the OS and Windows 3.*x* for the GUI. Windows 95 provides both the OS and the GUI.

DOS

The installation process places the system files on the root directory of the primary disk drive; creates a directory for the external DOS commands, drivers, and utilities; then expands the files off the floppy installation disk and into the directory on the hard drive. A bootable disk requires that the IO.SYS system file be placed in the first sector of the primary disk drive and that the partition be designated as the active partition.

To install DOS on a machine, the machine must be an IBM or compatible system (8086/8088 or later). To verify the type of system you have, you can look at the documentation that came with it or (on most AT-based machines) watch the boot-up screens—one of them will tell you the type of processor it has. An IBM-compatible computer will have a CPU based on the 8088 chip (80286, 80386, 80486, 80586, 80686) or the Pentium chip.

You must also have between 4 and 5 megabytes (depending on the version you are installing and whether you perform a full installation) of available disk space on your disk drive.

Installation is a straightforward process. You insert the first installation disk into drive A:, then perform either a cold boot (turn the computer off then on) or a warm boot (Ctrl+Alt+Shift). An alternate way to start the installation process is to type **A: SETUP** or **A: INSTALL** at the command prompt after inserting the installation disk into the A: drive.

NOTE   The disk drive must be partitioned before you can start installing DOS, but it does not have to be formatted. If the disk is not formatted, the SETUP utility will do it for you.

The majority of the installation is done automatically with the system prompting you to change diskettes as needed. During the process, you will be prompted to verify or change some of the default values assumed by the utility. Some of the items you will have to verify are as follows:

- The type of video on your system

- The type of keyboard being used

- The type of computer you are using

- The directory in which you want to place DOS

Unless you are installing the system on a computer that will be used by non-U.S. citizens, the majority of these default values will be OK. However, read the installation screens carefully to determine that what is being presented is really what you need to have done.

NOTE Most DOS installations can be completed within five to 10 minutes.

Windows 3.x

Once DOS has been installed, you will need to install Windows 3.x. It is usually best to install Windows immediately after the OS to avoid any conflicts with TSRs or other system variables that may be set by other applications. If you plan on compressing your disk, Windows should be placed in a noncompressed portion of your disk or on a separate partition.

According to Microsoft, you will need the following minimum requirements to install Windows 3.x:

- MS-DOS version 3.1 or later (or its PC DOS or DRDOS equivalent)

- An 80286 or later processor

- 1MB total memory

- A high-density floppy disk drive

- At least 5 to 12MB free space on your hard disk (depending on the version you install, the method of installation, and what is installed)

- An EGA or better video card and monitor

- A serial or bus mouse

NOTE The minimum requirements listed by Microsoft are for marketing purposes only. They do not reflect real-world needs at all.

As you leave the idealistic laboratory and its perfect conditions for the real world of human usage, the minimum requirements change to the following, more realistic criteria:

- DOS version 5 or later

- An 80386 or better CPU (this CPU's Protected mode allows Windows to use its multi-tasking feature)

- 4MB RAM—8MB are better; 16MB are optimal. Significant increases in performance can be seen up to 16MB. Having more than 16MB RAM does help, but does not give the tremendous performance boosts seen with upgrades to the 16MB level.

- At least 40MB of available hard disk space. Keep in mind that you will need hard disk space to act as virtual memory, for spooling print jobs onto the disk, and to hold various variables and information that Windows places in its TEMP directory.

- A high-density 3.5-inch floppy disk drive

- An SVGA card and monitor capable of 800×600 resolution

- A Microsoft-compatible mouse

This installation process is also fairly simple and straightforward. You insert disk one of the installation disks into drive A:, change to A:, and type **SETUP** at the command prompt.

SETUP starts up in DOS mode, evaluates your system, looks for other copies of Windows, then asks for verification of the following data:

- The directory where you want Windows loaded

- The type of computer

- The type of video display that you are using

- The type of mouse/pointing device being used

- The type of keyboard and language layout

- The type of network

- The type of printer and the I/O port to which it is connected

- The name and company name

- The names of the applications you wish to run from Windows icons

Typically, the default values selected by SETUP will be the best ones for your system. Pay close attention to the installation screens and make changes to the default values as needed.

After it analyzes the system, Windows copies an initial set of files to the hard disk, then boots itself into Windows mode and finishes the installation with a GUI interface. If you are having trouble with Windows locking up at this point, it is because SETUP cannot recognize one or more pieces of hardware on the system.

Restart the installation process using SETUP /I at the command line. This makes the entire installation process interactive. You will be prompted to supply all of the information about your system that Windows would normally find itself.

If you are installing Windows on a network such as Novell, you would use the SETUP /A command to place files on the server, from which you can then install them on workstations.

As the installation progresses, you will be prompted to change diskettes. If you insert the wrong disk, the system will merely prompt you to insert the correct disk again.

The only tricky parts of the installation are selecting and setting up the printers and network environments, which are covered in other sections of this book.

If you do not get the correct hardware during the initial installation, you can run SETUP at any time to make any necessary changes. You will also want to run it if you experience problems with a network card or printer. Users are notorious for messing with system settings and may have selected a wrong device driver or protocol.

NOTE   Installing Windows 3.*x* usually requires around 20 to 30 minutes to complete.

Windows 95

Windows 95 is a complete operating system and GUI all built into one program. Just like any other operating system, the disk drive needs to be partitioned before you start.

Installation media can be either diskette or CD-ROM. Using diskettes to install the operating system is much the same as for loading Windows 3.*x* or DOS. If you use the CD-ROM, you will have to boot the system into DOS first. For the CD-ROM to be recognized, the CD-ROM driver must be called from CONFIG.SYS, and the MSCDEX.EXE utility must be called from AUTOEXEC.BAT. The appropriate CD-ROM driver and the MSCDEX.EXE files must be located on the disk from which you boot.

NOTE   Many installation setups come with a diskette that will have the appropriate drivers and files already on it. This diskette is used to boot the computer and set up the CD-ROM. If you do not have such a disk, you can create one by making a bootable disk with the CD-ROM driver and MSCDEX.EXE on it. You will also have to create a CONFIG.SYS file that will activate the CD-ROM driver and an AUTOEXEC.BAT file that will launch the MSCDEX.EXE file.

To take maximum advantage of Windows 95's PnP feature, you should install all of your hardware first. This will allow the installation program to determine all of the hardware components on your system and install all of the Windows 95 drivers that it needs to support the system. Otherwise, you will have to use the installation media each time you install a new piece of hardware.

According to Microsoft, Windows 95 requires

- A 386DX CPU

- 4MB of RAM

- 35 to 40MB of available disk space

- A VGA card and monitor

- A serial or bus mouse

- A standard keyboard

The minimum real-world application requires the following items:

- A 486DX33—Pentium is better

- 16MB of RAM—32MB are better

- An SVGA card and monitor

- A serial or parallel mouse

- A standard keyboard—a Windows 95 keyboard is better

Installing Windows 95 is best accomplished on a machine that has all of the hardware already installed in it, with no software. If you are doing a CD-ROM installation, you will need a boot disk with the CD drivers and a utility designed for your CD player.

The diskette installation takes the same basic form as the DOS/ Windows 3.*x* installation. You start with disk one and insert the additional diskettes as prompted.

Windows 95 makes installation a bit more user friendly by providing an Installation Wizard that does most of the work for you. The

Wizard will prompt you to answer a few questions regarding where you want the Windows 95 directory, your name and company, the product identification number, and any devices that you may have on your system that it could not identify. Your name and the product ID are required entries.

The CD-ROM installation is much easier. Once you boot your computer and activate the CD player, you insert the Windows 95 CD-ROM into the player, change to the CD drive, and type in **SETUP**.

During the installation process, you are given a choice for performing a typical, portable, compact, or custom installation.

- The *typical* installation will install what Microsoft thinks is the most popular features of Windows 95.

- The *portable* installation will install the most needed features for portable computers.

- The *compact* installation will install the bare minimum features of Windows 95.

- The *custom* installation allows you to pick and choose which features you want on your system.

The installation process will also ask you whether you want to create a start-up disk. It is highly recommended that you do so. In addition, you will need to periodically copy the USER.DAT and SYSTEM.DAT files onto this disk so that you will have a current copy of the files needed to rebuild your Registry.

NOTE The time it takes to install Windows 95 depends upon the method you use and the speed of your system and CD player. If you use diskettes on a slower system, it will take 30 to 60 minutes. With a CD player, you will spend around 20 to 30 minutes.

Installing the Appropriate Drivers

Unless you have some proprietary equipment, Windows 95 supplies most of the drivers and hardware utilities needed for your system. If you have DOS/Windows 3.*x* programs that require special drivers, you will have to insert these drivers into the CONFIG .SYS, AUTOEXEC.BAT, WIN.INI, and/or SYSTEM.INI files where they would normally be inserted under DOS/Windows 3.*x*. Otherwise, Windows 95 does not need these files.

DOS

The most important drivers for DOS are listed below.

CONFIG.SYS: Device drivers can be loaded into conventional memory using the DEVICE= command and into upper memory with the DEVICEHIGH= command. The following device drivers are used with DOS-based programs and hardware:

- **ANSI.SYS:** Provides enhanced capability for DOS-based graphics used through batch files.

- **CD-ROM driver:** Provides the hardware interface for the CD-ROM device. The CD player manufacturer usually supplies this driver.

- **DBLSPACE.SYS:** Used to move DoubleSpace into upper memory. Available in version 6 and later.

- **EMM386.EXE:** Provides upper memory support and management as well as expanded memory support. Available in version 5 and later.

- **HIMEM.SYS:** Provides extended memory support. Available in version 5 and later. This is the only device driver that cannot be loaded into upper memory and must be listed before the DEVICEHIGH command can be used. It must also be used before EMM386.EXE.

- **RAMDRIVE:** Creates a disk drive out of RAM and simulates a regular hard disk drive.

- **SETVER.EXE:** Tricks older DOS-based programs, which require a specific version of DOS, into running on a later version.

- **SMARTDRV.EXE:** Creates a disk cache in extended or expanded memory. Available only in versions 4 and 5.

- A typical CONFIG.SYS file includes

```
device=c:\dos\himem.sys
device=c:\dos\emm386.exe noems
dos=high,umb
buffers=12
files=30
stacks=0,0
shell=c:\dos\command.com c:\dos /e:256 /p
devicehigh=c:\cdrom\cddrv.sys /d:cd001
devicehigh c:\dos\setver.exe
devicehigh=c:\mouse\mouse.sys
devicehigh=c:\windows\ramdrive.sys 1024 /e
devicehigh=smartdrv.exe
```

AUTOEXEC.BAT: The following list consists of command utilities used extensively by DOS.

- **DOSKEY.EXE:** Provides a DOS command editor and the ability to create keyboard macros.

- **FASTOPEN.EXE:** This is really a command, but it sets up disk caching for DOS.

- **MSCDEX.EXE:** This is a command, but it is necessary for CD players that do not come with their own support utility.

- **SMARTDRV.EXE:** Newer version supplied by DOS 6 and Windows 3.1. SMARTDRV creates a disk cache in extended memory. This utility can be loaded in either CONFIG.SYS or AUTOEXEC.BAT, but not both. If you are using DOS 5 and later, it should be activated in the AUTOEXEC.BAT file.

- A typical AUTOEXEC.BAT file includes

```
@echo off
prompt=$p$g
set temp=c:\temp
path=c:\windows;c:\dos;d:\msoffice
c:\dos\mscdex.exe /d:cd001 /m:10
c:\dos\mirror c: /tc
c:\windows\smartdrv.exe
```

Windows 3.x

The most important drivers and utilities needed by Windows 3.*x* are as follows:

> **DOS:** Windows needs the same drivers as DOS. If a driver is beneficial in DOS, it is helpful to Windows 3.*x* as well. If a driver is located in both the DOS and the Windows directory, go with the later version as indicated by the date of the file.
>
> - HIMEM.SYS must be installed in CONFIG.SYS before Windows will work.
>
> - EMM386.EXE is not essential, but it does help to manage memory resources. At times, EMM386 will interfere with Windows and require you to experiment with the include and exclude switches that accompany EMM386.
>
> **WIN.INI:** Although it's not a driver in itself, Windows uses WIN.INI to load many of the system drivers and OS parameters required.
>
> **SYSTEM.INI:** This is another file that loads system parameters and device drivers for the Windows environment.

Windows 95

Windows 95 takes all of the necessary drivers and utilities, and incorporates them into the operating system or makes them a part of the Registry. The basic files needed for the Registry are as follows:

> **USER.DAT:** This file contains the basic information for the user, such as the screen settings and other user-interface parameters.
>
> **SYSTEM.DAT:** This file contains information about the setup of the system, such as the name and location of all the devices on the system and the appropriate device driver needed to run them.

The Registry is re-created every time Windows 95 is rebooted.

NOTE The CONFIG.SYS, AUTOEXEC.BAT, WIN.INI, and SYSTEM
.INI files are used only when you have an application that runs in the
DOS/Windows 3.*x* environment. They will be included in your system
for backward compatibility only. If you are using only 32-bit programs
that are specifically written for Windows 95, you will not have these
files on your system.

Using Text Editors to Modify CONFIG.SYS and AUTOEXEC.BAT

Editing the system files that configure your system is an essential part of
maintaining a computer system. Knowing which utilities to use and
how to use them are important for keeping your system working at an
optimal level. There are many different methods of editing these system
files—you can use anything from a line editor to a full-blown word processor. All the editor has to do is save the file in ASCII text format.

In most cases, you will use a text editor to create and modify your
system files. The two most common text editors are EDIT in DOS
and NOTEPAD in Windows 3.*x* and Windows 95. Many third-
party editors are also available that are far superior to those provided by Microsoft with their OS. However, for most practical purposes, unless you are a programmer, you do not need them. The ones
provided by Microsoft are more than adequate for modifying
system files.

The only ASCII text processor available with DOS is EDIT.COM. It
is a basic screen editor that relies on the source-code editor built into
QBASIC. You must have QBASIC installed to use EDIT. To use EDIT,
type **EDIT** at the command prompt. EDIT gives you a basic text processor without any enhanced print or formatting features.

When working with Windows 3.*x* or Windows 95, you can use
NOTEPAD. NOTEPAD is a Windows-based text processor that has
the added advantage of copying text onto the Clipboard and pasting

it into another file. To use NOTEPAD, double-click its icon in the Main program group; locate it in the WINDOWS directory with the File Manager and double-click its filename (NOTEPAD.EXE); or type **NOTEPAD** in the dialog box for the Start ➤ Run option off the menu bar. NOTEPAD gives you a basic text editor without the enhanced print or formatting features.

Using SYSEDIT to Modify CONFIG.SYS and AUTOEXEC.BAT

In both Windows 3.*x* and Windows 95, you have a utility called SYSEDIT. As shown in Figure 3.1, SYSEDIT is a multi-windowed text processor that works just like NOTEPAD.

FIGURE 3.1: SYSEDIT

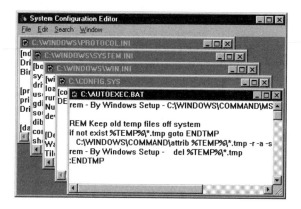

EDIT loads CONFIG.SYS, AUTOEXEC.BAT, WIN.INI, and SYSTEM.INI into separate windows on the desktop. You can then edit each of them in turn without having to load and save each one separately. You can easily move between the files just by clicking the window of the file on which you want to work.

Necessary Procedures

You need to basically understand the steps required for getting the disk drive ready for use, installing the operating system, and upgrading the operating system. Be sure you know the terminology and location of each of the functions you need to access.

SEE ALSO Due to the nature of this book, these procedures will be covered in a general-overview manner, touching lightly on the more pertinent subject matter. For a more detailed approach, please refer to the installation guide or one of the many other books about the subject, such as *A+ Windows/DOS Study Guide* by David Groth, published by Sybex.

Preparing the Disk Drive for Use

Preparing a hard disk for use involves partitioning the disk drive and formatting each of the partitions you created.

1. Partition the hard disk drive using the FDISK utility (the FDISK menu is shown below). At a minimum, you must set a primary DOS partition. If needed, you can create up to three additional partitions as extended DOS partitions. You can then designate each of the extended partitions as logical drives.

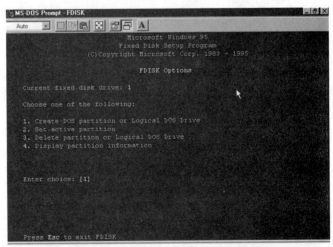

NOTE DOS allows a maximum of four partitions on a hard drive and a maximum of 26 physical and/or logical disk drives.

2. Next, you need to set an active partition. Return to the FDISK menu and select option two. Enter **1** at the prompt for the partition selection to set the primary DOS partition to active.

3. At the FDISK menu, select option four to view what you have set up.

NOTE If you have to modify the partition structures at this time, you can use option three from the main menu and delete the partitions as needed.

4. Press Esc again to exit FDISK. You will then be prompted to insert a system disk into drive A: and to press any key to continue. This will reboot your system and display the command prompt.

5. Type in **FORMAT C:/S** to format the primary partition/disk drive. This will prepare the disk drive for use by placing the tracks and sectors, and creating the FAT.

6. Type **FORMAT** *drive*: at the DOS prompt for each of the logical drives you created while partitioning the drive. The drive will be the letter of the logical drive.

NOTE Most DOS installation disks are happier if they find an active partition without an operating system already installed. DOS upgrade programs require you to have an older version of the operating system already on the system. If you are using an upgrade, you can use either a SYS or a FORMAT /S command to put the OS on the disk. Just make sure this version is older than the one you will be installing.

Installing DOS

Once the drive has been formatted, the next step in getting a system operational is to install the operating system.

1. Partition the drive.

2. Turn off the computer, insert disk one of the installation disks into drive A:, and turn the computer back on.

3. Change diskettes as prompted.

NOTE The DOS installation program will automatically format the drive if it hasn't already been done.

---

4. After the installation has been completed, you need to check the AUTOEXEC.BAT file and verify all the settings made by the installation program.

NOTE DOS 6 has a tendency to place the system's temporary files into the DOS directory. To prevent possible problems, you should create a TEMP directory on C: (C:\TEMP) and change the SET TEMP= C:\DOS entry in AUTOEXEC.BAT to read SET TEMP=C:\TEMP.

---

5. To bring the system up to minimal operating standards, you must now install all the device drivers for your hardware, such as scanners, mouse, and CD player.

Installing Windows 3.x

After DOS has been installed, you need to set up the user interface. In most cases, Windows 3.x will be the GUI of choice for DOS-based systems.

If you have a choice, you should install Windows 3.x immediately after installing DOS. It makes the installation of software easier and eliminates some of the problems associated with TSRs and system variables.

If you are using disk compression software, you should keep Windows out of the compressed files. Compressing them will slow your system down.

1. Insure that DOS has been installed on your system.

2. Insert disk one of the installation disk set into drive A:. Change to the A: drive and type in **SETUP** at the command prompt. The screen will tell you to wait while it checks out the system hardware. After a few moments, the welcome screen will appear. Press Enter to continue.

3. You will then be prompted for Express or Custom setup.

   ■ Express setup is recommended. It will automatically configure your mouse, keyboard, language, and network, and modify AUTOEXEC.BAT and CONFIG.SYS. It also installs the applications, utilities, and drivers Microsoft believes to be the most popular and necessary for the typical system. It will assume you wish to install any applications that are already loaded.

   ■ Custom setup will require you to verify DOS settings, enter user information, and then select the components you wish to have loaded. You can select only those Windows components (applets and utilities) that you feel you need on your system. Custom setup also lets you configure your virtual-memory parameters, and determine whether to install printer drivers and DOS programs into Windows groups.

4. The final step in the installation procedure is to install your print drivers.

Reboot the system, verify the modifications in the AUTOEXEC.BAT and CONFIG.SYS files, then reboot the computer. The Windows environment should be up to minimum standards at this time.

NOTE You can use a Windows utility called SYSEDIT that will automatically load the following files: AUTOEXEC.BAT, CONFIG.SYS, SYSTEM.INI, and WIN.INI. With these files loaded, you can make modifications as needed. To optimize DOS programs for Windows, you can use the PIF Editor to set the parameters for any particular DOS-based application or utility. To configure the desktop and operational features of Windows to meet your preferences and system needs, you can use the Control Panel.

Installing Windows 95

Windows 95 gives you a single installation of both the operating system and the user interface. The installation program comes on a CD-ROM that greatly simplifies installation.

It is recommended that you install all of the hardware you are planning on using in the system before installing Windows 95. While PnP is supposed to work the same every time you boot your system, experience has shown the best time for PnP to work is at the time of installation.

1. Boot your computer with the boot disk.

NOTE Installing Windows 95 on a new disk drive requires that you have the device drivers for the CD player and MSCDEX.EXE on your boot diskette. The appropriate entries must be made in CONFIG.SYS (e.g., device=c:\cdrom\cd_drv.sys) and AUTOEXEC.BAT (e.g., c:\dos\ mscdex /d: c:\cd_drv.sys /L:D).

2. Insert the Windows 95 CD in the CD player, change to the CD drive, and enter **SETUP** at the command line.

3. The installation process has three major stages:

   - **Information collection:** You will be prompted for the Windows directory, type of installation, user name, company information, and the product ID. The system also prompts you for your e-mail options, the components you want installed, and a start-up disk. Then, the system analyzes your hardware setup.

NOTE   A progress bar will be displayed on your screen. If it stops moving for more than 10 minutes without any activity from your hard disk, the machine is probably locked up. Reboot the system and rerun SETUP. SETUP will take up where it left off.

- **File copy and expansion:** This section copies all the OS components you wanted and the necessary drivers for the hardware it detected.

- **Finalizing the setup:** This final step displays the Finishing Setup screen. To finish the setup, click the Finish button. The system will reboot and prepare Windows 95 to run for the first time. During this time, it will create the icons and generate the settings necessary for the Registry—it finishes with you setting the time zone. Then, the computer will reboot one more time—the installation is completed.

Exam Essentials

The exam features a can-do approach to installation. This means that you should be quite familiar with the installation processes, the locations of the selection features in the installation procedures, and the sequencing of the screens needed to perform the installations. You should also be familiar with the different switches used with the commands located in CONFIG.SYS and AUTOEXEC.BAT, and have a basic understanding of the different sections used in the SYSTEM.INI and WIN.INI files.

Know which text editor to use for editing system files.   EDIT is the only text editor in DOS. If you do not have Windows installed, you must use EDIT. EDIT relies on QBASIC for its editing abilities. SYSEDIT is the editor of choice with Windows 3.*x* and Windows 95 when you have to work on all four of the system files at one time. NOTEPAD is the editor of choice when you have only one Windows 3.*x* or Windows 95 system file to modify.

Know what to do if you use a regular word processor to modify system files. If you do use a word processor to modify the ASCII system files, save the files as ASCII text files. If you don't, the OS will not be able to read them.

Be familiar with the most commonly used command lines located in the DOS CONFIG.SYS file and how to load them into memory. The most common drivers loaded by CONFIG.SYS include HIMEM.SYS, EMM386.EXE, and SETVER.EXE. The DEVICE= command loads the drivers into conventional memory, and DEVICEHIGH= loads them into upper memory blocks (UMBs).

Be familiar with the most commonly used command lines in the DOS AUTOEXEC.BAT. The common command lines used in the AUTOEXEC.BAT file include the PROMPT, SET, and PATH commands. Loading memory-resident utilities (TSRs) requires a command line that lists the path and the filename. To load them into UMBs, use the LOADHIGH or LH command in front of the path name. Launching a regular program is the same as loading TSRs. Programs are usually listed after the TSRs have been loaded.

Know the basic requirements to install the DOS operating system on a new hard drive. To bring a new hard drive up to minimum operational standards, you must partition the hard drive, format the hard drive, install the OS, and configure the system to user needs.

Be familiar with the most commonly used command lines located in the Windows 3.x CONFIG.SYS file. HIMEM.SYS is required for Windows to run. EMM386.EXE can cause problems, but can also make a significant positive impact on memory management. RAMDRIVE.SYS can be used to boost performance by designating the RAM disk for temporary and swap files.

Know the basic system requirements for Windows 3.x installation. There is a difference between marketing information and real-world application. Marketing suggests Windows needs a 386 CPU, 1MB RAM, an EGA video card and monitor, DOS 3.1, and 10 to 12MB free disk space. Real-world requirements for Windows 3.x include a 486 CPU, 8MB RAM, SVGA video card, DOS 5 or later, and a large enough hard drive to contain the OS, all of your applications, and the swap file. For the exam, you should be able to answer questions for both marketing and real-world requirements.

Be familiar with the most commonly used command lines located in the Windows 95 CONFIG.SYS and AUTOEXEC.BAT files. Windows 95 does not require these files unless you are running legacy programs that require their own drivers and utilities to operate. The Windows 95 OS and the Registry have absorbed these files. Drivers are loaded through the New Hardware Installation Wizard.

Know the basic system requirements for Windows 95 installation. Again, there is a difference between the real-world and marketing requirements for Windows 95. Marketing hype states that you can use a 386, 4MB RAM, 35 to 40MB of available disk space, and a VGA video card and monitor. Real-world requirements indicate a Pentium 133 CPU, 32MB RAM, and an SVGA monitor.

Key Terms and Concepts

Active partition: The partition on a hard drive that the system looks in for the OS boot files. This is usually the primary DOS partition on the disk drive.

ANSI.SYS: A CONFIG.SYS driver that allows for screen graphics using DOS batch files.

DBLSPACE.SYS: The driver that provides disk compression for the system. This utility is available in DOS 6 and DOS 6.20—in DOS 6.21, there is no driver; in DOS 6.22, the compression driver is called DRVSPACE.SYS.

Extended DOS partition: A DOS partition other than the primary DOS partition. See also *Partition* and *Primary DOS partition*.

FDISK.EXE: The DOS command used to partition a hard disk drive.

FORMAT.EXE: The DOS command that creates the FAT and prepares the disk for use.

Line editor: A very basic type of text editor that will allow the user to create and modify only one line of text at a time. Once you press Enter, you cannot go back and change the preceding line.

Logical disk drive: A drive letter designation assigned to an extended DOS partition.

MSCDEX.EXE: The Microsoft CD-ROM extension to DOS. It allows users to connect CD players to their systems.

OEM (original equipment manufacturer): The term is applied to components that you buy from a supplier usually without partitions or formatting.

Partition: A division of the hard drive. There can be up to four partitions on a single drive. The drive must have a partition and the resulting partition table before it can be seen by the OS.

Primary DOS partition: The first partition on the hard disk drive.

Primary drive: The first drive in the hard-disk-drive chain. On DOS computers, this would be the C: drive.

RAMDISK.SYS: A CONFIG.SYS driver used to set up a virtual hard disk in RAM.

Screen editor: A more versatile text editor that allows the user to create and modify text anywhere within the document. Once you press Enter to go to the next line, you can still return to any other previous line and make whatever changes are necessary.

SETUP.EXE: The DOS command that activates almost all of Microsoft's installation utilities.

SETVER.EXE: A DOS command that makes older DOS-based programs think that the newer DOS version is the version they need to work.

SMARTDRV.EXE: The DOS command used to activate a disk cache. Older versions were used in CONFIG.SYS, and newer ones were activated through AUTOEXEC.BAT.

Text editor: An editor that works with ASCII text characters only. It can work with alphabetic and numeric characters, but cannot be used for anything besides simple text entry.

Wizard: A GUI utility that walks users through whichever process it was designed for (e.g., the Setup Wizard and New Hardware Installation Wizard).

Sample Questions

1. Which command is entered at the DOS prompt to start a normal Windows 95 installation?

   A. Load

   B. Install

   C. Setup

   D. Setup /I

   Answer: C. The SETUP.EXE command is used to activate the normal installation utilities for DOS, Windows 3.*x*, and Windows 95.

2. HIMEM.SYS is used within which file to set up extended memory for DOS?

   A. WIN.INI

   B. AUTOEXEC.BAT

   C. SYSTEM.INI

   D. CONFIG.SYS

   Answer: D. HIMEM.SYS is a device driver, and CONFIG.SYS is normally used to load device drivers in DOS.

3. Which editor would you use to edit all four of the ASCII system files in Windows 3.*x*?

   A. WORDPAD

   B. NOTEPAD

C. EDIT

D. SYSEDIT

Answer: D. SYSEDIT is a utility that can be used to work on CONFIG.SYS, AUTOEXEC.BAT, WIN.INI, and COMMAND .COM as a group.

4. Which text editor would you use to edit system files on a DOS-based machine?

A. WORDPAD

B. NOTEPAD

C. EDIT

D. SYSEDIT

Answer: C. EDIT.COM is the only editor available under DOS.

Identify steps to perform an operating system upgrade.

The focus of this objective is on the procedures and other elements required to perform system upgrades to Windows 95. Since the vast majority of computers already have operating systems (DOS and Windows 3.x), it is imperative that you know what is involved in upgrading a machine based on a legacy operating system to Windows 95.

Critical Information

Upgrading from DOS or Windows 3.1 to Windows 95 is almost like an initial installation on a new disk drive. You go through the same basic steps:

- Gathering information about the system

- Copying files to the computer

- Finishing the setup routine

Since the upgrade process is nearly identical to the initial installation process, only the major areas of difference will be covered in the upgrades for DOS and Windows 3.*x*.

Upgrading from DOS to Windows 95

Upgrading from DOS to Windows 95 gives you the option of saving your original OS. To do this, you need to indicate your desire during the information-gathering portion of installation.

You are advised to keep your original OS if you have any DOS applications that directly access hardware components. These types of programs are incompatible with Windows 95 (they are usually action games that require immediate access to hardware devices to increase their speed).

If you do decide to keep your original OS, you can access it by pressing F8 during the boot up to get the Windows 95 menu, then selecting the Previous Version option. The upgrade procedures modify the AUTOEXEC.BAT and CONFIG.SYS files to meet the new requirements of the system under Windows 95.

Upgrading from Windows 3.*x* to Windows 95

Upgrading from Windows 3.*x* to Windows 95 is basically like the other installation methods. To keep your original Windows 3.*x* system available for use, you can assign Windows 95 to another directory (e.g., WIN95). This will allow Windows 3.*x* to remain untouched in the Windows directory.

During the information-gathering process, you will be asked whether you wish to save the existing system files. If you answer in the affirmative, the DOS and Windows files will be duplicated. This action requires an additional 6MB of disk space and is a good idea in case the installation fails or the system doesn't work after the installation. With the duplicate files, you can easily uninstall Windows 95 and restore your system to the same state it was in prior to the installation. If everything works after the installation, the duplicate files can be deleted to recover the disk space.

NOTE Many people have reported problems with upgrading from Windows 3.x to Windows 95 when they install Windows 95 into the same directory as Windows 3.x. The system becomes unstable. Sometimes the problems surface immediately, and sometimes it takes a month or so. It will be to your long-term advantage to install Windows 95 into a separate directory to avoid these possible problems.

The CONFIG.SYS and AUTOEXEC.BAT files are modified during the upgrade process to meet the needs of your system under Windows 95.

Loading the Appropriate Drivers

The best procedure for installing device drivers is to install all the hardware you want on the system before you install Windows 95. The SETUP utility searches the system for the hardware that is on it, selects the appropriate drivers, and loads them automatically during the installation process.

Installing device drivers after Windows 95 has been installed requires you to use the New Hardware Installation Wizard. Select the Add New Hardware option in the Control Panel to activate the Wizard. The Control Panel is accessed either through the My Computer folder on the desktop or by selecting Start ➤ Settings.

Necessary Procedures

The only procedure that needs to be reviewed at this point is the one to add new device drivers. The upgrade process is very similar to the initial installation covered in an earlier section on installation procedures.

Installing Drivers for New Hardware into Windows 95

Driver installation in Windows 95 is a fairly straightforward process provided you have PnP devices. Otherwise, it can be time consuming as you set and test various patterns of IRQ, DMA, and port address values.

1. Choose Start ➤ Settings ➤ Control Panel.

2. Double-click the Add New Hardware icon. This will display the Add New Hardware Wizard, as shown below.

3. Let the Add New Hardware Wizard find the new hardware, or do it manually.

   ▪ In the automated installation, the Wizard will search the system for new hardware and select the appropriate driver for it. If the driver is not in the vast arsenal of drivers available to Windows, it will prompt you to insert the Windows 95 CD-ROM or the diskette with the driver on it. This installation is best since it adds the device to the Device Manager database.

   ▪ The manual installation should be used only when the Wizard is unable to identify the device you have installed. The manual routine requires that you name the device's manufacturer and model. If Windows 95 does not have a suitable device, it will prompt you for either the CD-ROM or the manufacturer's diskette.

Exam Essentials

The exam will test your understanding of the upgrade process. You should make sure you are familiar with the actual upgrade process and how it is different from an initial installation. There will also be questions dealing with the process of installing or reinstalling drivers after the installation/upgrade process has been completed.

Know how to add new hardware to your system.   After you have installed the new hardware device into your system, you need to run the Add New Hardware utility in the Control Panel. Double-click this icon to start the Add New Hardware Wizard. You can either install the device driver manually or have the Wizard do it for you.

NOTE   It is recommended that you let the Wizard do it for you—especially if the device is PnP. Perform a manual installation only if the Wizard cannot recognize your device. The manual installation accepts what you have entered and does not verify the settings. Your first indication that the manual installation did not succeed is after you have rebooted your system and the new device doesn't work.

After the installation, you must restart your computer before the new device can be used. During the reboot sequence, Windows 95 will create the necessary entries in the Registry.

Key Terms and Concepts

AUTOEXEC.BAT: The DOS system file used to load TSRs into memory and set system parameters.

CONFIG.SYS: The DOS system file that controls the general system environment and is used to load device drivers.

Control Panel: The Windows component that the user uses to customize the look and operation of the system.

Device driver: Software that is used to help the system communicate with a device in the most optimal manner.

DoubleSpace: The disk compression utility shipped with DOS 6.22 and Windows 95.

FILES=:   The CONFIG.SYS command that determines how many files the OS can have open at one time.

Legacy software: Operating systems, utilities, and applications based on the 16-bit DOS operating system. Any program created for DOS or Windows 3.*x*.

Registry: The centralized database used by Windows for environmental settings.

Upgrade: A method of enhancing a system with a newer version of a software package by purchasing an add-on package. Normally, upgrades require the presence of an authorized version before they can be used.

Wizard: A part of the Windows 95 GUI that presents itself as an on-screen guide that takes the user step by step through the process it was designed to perform.

Sample Questions

1. How do you install a device driver for a new piece of hardware?

    A. Through the Devices option in the Control Panel

    B. Through the System option in the Control Panel

    C. Through the Add New Software option in the Control Panel

    D. Through the Add New Hardware option in the Control Panel

    Answer: D. The Add New Hardware option in the Control Panel is where new device drivers are added.

2. The upgrade process leaves the AUTOEXEC.BAT and CONFIG.SYS files alone. True or false?

Answer: False. The files are left there, but are modified to meet the new criteria of Windows 95.

Identify the basic system boot sequences and alternative ways to boot the system software, including the steps to create an emergency boot disk with utilities installed.

This objective concentrates on the boot-up process. You will have to know the order in which the system files are called into operation and what can be done to modify the normal boot sequence.

Critical Information

The information contained in this section is critical for troubleshooting and diagnosing boot-up problems. You should know and understand what the system does and how it does it so that you can effectively analyze boot-up problems and resolve them in a timely manner.

The DOS Boot-Up Sequence

After the POST has been performed, the system BIOS activates the boot kernel, which then starts loading the OS into memory. The DOS boot-up sequence is as follows:

IO.SYS: A hidden file in the root directory of the primary partition of the primary drive. It provides the basic input/output capabilities for the system. IO.SYS gives the system its ability to communicate with the system peripheral devices. It also directs the overall process of loading the OS.

MSDOS.SYS: A hidden file in the root directory that comprises the major portion of the OS. It is often called the kernel. This file is responsible for receiving requests for service from the applications and translating these requests into actions for IO.SYS to perform.

CONFIG.SYS: A text file that normally contains device drivers and system setup values.

COMMAND.COM: The COMMAND.COM file is the user interface. This file accepts requests from the user, launches programs, and passes commands to MSDOS.SYS.

AUTOEXEC.BAT: A text file used to set system variables and load TSRs.

When the computer is turned on, the system performs a power on self test (POST), and if all is well, it triggers the ROM BIOS routine. The BIOS looks for and loads the master boot record (MBR), which contains data on how the hard disk drive is partitioned. The MBR runs the partition table program, which is designed to locate the bootable drive and load the IO.SYS file into memory. If the MBR cannot find IO.SYS, it displays the "Missing Operating System" error message. If it finds it, it loads it into memory.

Once IO.SYS is loaded into memory, it initializes its set of device drivers to communicate with the hardware and then calls an internal routine called SYSINIT. SYSINIT controls the rest of the boot process. SYSINIT loads MSDOS.SYS into memory and verifies that it has loaded properly. Finally, it locates CONFIG.SYS and starts loading the device drivers and configuration options that are not part of the base IO.SYS file.

IO.SYS also contains pointers to the MSDOS.SYS and COMMAND .COM files. When the commands in CONFIG.SYS have all been processed, SYSINIT loads the command interpreter defined by the SHELL= line in the CONFIG.SYS file, usually COMMAND.COM.

Once COMMAND.COM is loaded, it takes over the system. Its first function is to locate the AUTOEXEC.BAT file and execute the command lines it finds there. If it does not find an AUTOEXEC.BAT file, it executes the DATE and TIME commands. The final action in the boot-up process is when COMMAND.COM displays the DOS prompt.

NOTE The boot-up process for PC-DOS (the operating system created by IBM) runs the following sequence: The boot record loads IBMBIO.COM and IBMDOS.COM. IBMBIO then processes CONFIG .SYS and executes COMMAND.COM. COMMAND.COM then runs AUTOEXEC.BAT.

The Windows 3.x Boot-Up Sequence

After the DOS boot-up sequence has been accomplished, Windows 3.x can be loaded into memory. This can be done in two ways: you can enter WIN at the DOS prompt, or you can include it as the last line in the AUTOEXEC.BAT files.

WIN.COM is the loader program for Windows 3.x and loads the Windows system files in the following sequence:

KRNL386.EXE: The kernel's role is similar to that of IO.SYS—it handles the base operation functions such as memory management, file I/O, and application loading. The KRNL286.EXE and KRNL386.EXE files are located in the WINDOWS\SYSTEM directory.

GDI.EXE: The graphical device interface is responsible for graphics and printing. It is located in the WINDOWS\SYSTEM directory.

USER.GDI: The user interface is the input engine and provides the elements that handle the mouse, keyboard, and communication ports used with Windows. This file is located in the WINDOWS\ SYSTEM directory.

PROGMAN.EXE: The Program Manager is the final file in the Windows boot-up process. It provides the basic user interface (the desktop), from which all other actions in Windows must take place. It is located in the WINDOWS directory.

WIN.COM starts the loading sequence in Windows 3.*x* by displaying the Windows logo, checking the integrity of the Registry (REG.DAT), and checking to see whether there is enough memory, what processor is in the computer, and that HIMEM.SYS or another extended memory driver is loaded. Some of the other files involved in the boot up include:

WIN.INI: The Windows-initialization file provides the basic instructions to the OS that will set the Windows desktop environment. It is located in the WINDOWS directory.

SYSTEM.INI: The system-initialization file provides the instructions for customizing the OS's needs for hardware device drivers and other system events. It is located in the WINDOWS directory.

CONTROL.INI: The Control Panel–initialization file contains the settings for color schemes. In general, this file should not be modified manually. It is located in the WINDOWS directory.

PROGRAM.INI: The program-initialization file provides the system with information concerning the program icons and security restrictions. It is located in the WINDOWS directory.

WINFILE.INI: The Program Manager–initialization file provides the system with the information about the Program Manager's configuration. It is located in the WINDOWS directory.

The Windows 95 Boot-Up Sequence

The boot-up sequence for Windows 95 is a combination of the DOS and Windows 3.*x* sequences. The Windows 95 boot-up sequence is as follows:

IO.SYS: IO.SYS is the boot-up controller and starts the boot-up process by loading enough of a file system into memory that it can locate the other files it needs.

MSDOS.SYS: The MSDOS.SYS file is a hidden ASCII text file that contains information about the locations of the boot drive, root directory, start-up files, and Windows 95 directory. It contains information about the boot configuration parameters.

DRVSPACE.BIN: If a DRVSPACE.INI is present in the root directory, it provides the system with disk-compression capability, performs an integrity check on the SYSTEM.DAT file, loads SYSTEM.DAT, and loads a hardware profile from the Registry based on detected hardware.

CONFIG.SYS: If present, it provides a means of loading legacy drivers.

AUTOEXEC.BAT: If present, it provides the system with a way to load legacy utilities and TSRs.

VMM32.VxD: After AUTOEXEC.BAT is run, WIN.COM is automatically executed and loads VMM32.VxD. This is the virtual machine manager and loads other virtual device drivers as referenced in the Registry and SYSTEM.INI. After these files are loaded, WIN.COM switches the processor into Protected mode, initializes the devices, and loads the following files:

- **KERNEL32.DLL:** This file contains the majority of the OS code.

- **GDI.EXE/GDI32.DLL:** These files provide the graphics engine for both 16-bit and 32-bit graphics displays.

- **USER.EXE/USER32.DLL:** These files provide the user-interface engine and control the input for both 16-bit and 32-bit applications.

- **WIN.INI:** This file contains application information, and is used to load and configure programs.

- **DESKTOP:** The desktop is the basic user interface and replaces the Program Manager in Windows 3.*x*.

- **LOGON:** A dialog box that allows the user to enter their user name and password. It loads the user's profile, verifies access to the network, and runs any login scripts.

- **STARTUP Group:** This folder contains the programs you want to run automatically every time you boot the system.

After the system POST has been completed, the BIOS disables the PnP devices and maps them to appropriate IRQ, DMA, and I/O address resources. It then transfers control to the loader program. The loader switches the system to Real mode, then executes the master boot record (MBR) and IO.SYS.

IO.SYS processes the configuration data in MSDOS.SYS and displays the logo. If the drive is compressed, IO.SYS loads the appropriate compression driver, then selects a hardware profile from the Registry, loads the double-buffering drivers if needed, and processes CONFIG.SYS and AUTOEXEC.BAT if present.

IO.SYS then loads the virtual machine manager (VMM386.VxD). The VMM loads the virtual device drivers, switches to Protected mode, initializes and loads the external VxDs, and creates the hardware device tree.

The final stage of the boot-up process consists of loading the Windows 95 OS. The kernel (KERNEL32.DLL), graphics interface (GDI.EXE and GDI32.DLL), and user interface (USER.EXE and USER32.DLL) are executed. WIN.INI is processed to load and configure applications, and Explorer is run to initiate the Windows shell. Then, the desktop is loaded, and the Logon dialog box is displayed. The final action performed during the boot-up process is to execute the programs contained in the Startup group.

Boot-Up Strategies

Starting with DOS 6, Microsoft provided a means of allowing the user to create multiple boot-up procedures to tailor start-ups according to their needs.

DOS

DOS can be used to customize a boot-up sequence that is tailored to specific needs. This is accomplished through a combination of CONFIG.SYS and AUTOEXEC.BAT entries.

You can create a menu system in CONFIG.SYS that can be specially designed to load only certain drivers for specific events you wish to control. For instance, you can set up the menu to configure the computer as a networked workstation, an intelligent terminal to a mainframe, and as a stand-alone machine. With this setup, different users can use the same machine for different purposes. The AUTOEXEC.BAT file would also contain IF/THEN statements that further tailor the system to the specific needs.

Windows 95

Windows 95 also has a multi-boot capability. With Windows 95, you can boot into Windows 95 or a different OS. These options are available during the boot-up process. When the "Loading Windows 95" message is displayed, press F8. This will display the Windows 95 Startup menu with the following options:

Normal: This option allows Windows 95 to perform a regular boot up.

Logged: This option performs a normal boot up, but creates the BOOTLOG.TXT file, which keeps tab of each Windows component as it loads into memory.

Safe Mode: The Safe mode boots the OS without processing CONFIG.SYS and MSDOS.SYS. It loads only the absolute minimum of drivers the system needs for basic operations. This mode is used for troubleshooting the system and fixing any problems that occur. It is also the mode the OS defaults to when the computer is turned off without going through the shut-down process.

Step-by-Step Configuration: This option provides users with the ability to select only those drivers they want to load during the boot-up process. The OS will step the system through each driver and process that it loads prompting the user whether or not to load them. This mode is also used for troubleshooting the system.

Command Prompt Only: This option halts the boot up after the system has loaded everything it needs for Real-mode operation. This mode will put you into a general DOS environment that can be used to run DOS-only applications.

Safe Mode Command Prompt: This option is the same as Command Prompt Only, but does not process CONFIG.SYS or AUTOEXEC.BAT. This mode puts the computer into a generic DOS environment without any peripheral drivers. This mode is also used for troubleshooting the system and for those really pesky DOS applications that don't even get along with themselves.

Previous Version of MS-DOS: This option is available only if you performed an upgrade to a DOS-based system and opted to keep the original system active.

WARNING   If you use the Previous Version option, it can destroy the long filenames you are using in Windows 95.

You can also use a number of switches to load Windows 95 from the command prompt. These switches include:

/B—Boots Windows and creates the BOOTLOG.TXT file

/D:F—Disables the 32-bit Disk Access mode

/D:M—Boots the OS in Safe mode

/D:N—Boots the OS into Safe mode with network drivers loaded and ready for logging into the network

/D:S—Excludes Windows from using the memory address F000-FFFF

/D:V—Allows ROM to handle the hard-disk-drive interrupts

/D:X—Excludes the UMA from being used by the OS

Creating an Emergency Boot Disk

An emergency boot disk is an essential part of keeping your system alive and well. System crashes are an inevitable part of working with computers, and the emergency boot disk can help you recover from the majority of them with only a minor annoyance instead of a major catastrophe.

In DOS and Windows 3.x, you have to create your own emergency boot disk. This is accomplished by formatting a diskette and transferring the system files to it by using the FORMAT /S command or the SYS command on a formatted diskette. Either one of these processes creates a system boot disk that can be used to boot the system when the hard drive fails to boot.

To make the boot disk into an *emergency boot disk*, you need to copy the UNFORMAT, UNDELETE, SCANDISK, FDISK, FORMAT, SYS, MSD, and MEM commands to the disk. In addition, you need to copy a good antivirus program and a small but effective ASCII text editor. If part of your major installation takes place over a CD-ROM or a LAN, you will also need these files on your emergency boot disk. As you can see, your emergency boot disk may be two or three disks in size. One disk should have the boot-up files and a generic copy of the AUTOEXEC.BAT and CONFIG.SYS files, including only those commands and drivers that are needed for getting the system up and running.

To make a *recovery disk*, you will need a formatted diskette with the system boot-up files; a copy of any compressed file directories; and the system's CONFIG.SYS, AUTOEXEC.BAT, WIN.INI, and SYSTEM.INI files. In addition, you should have a copy of all your .GRP files for Windows.

Windows 95 has automated the process of creating an emergency boot disk and calls it a Startup Disk. To create a Startup Disk, go to the Control Panel, select Add/Remove Programs, and click the Startup Disk tab. Clicking the Create button will activate a Wizard that will walk you through the process of creating the Startup Disk. You will need a floppy disk in drive A: and access to your Windows 95 installation disks.

NOTE The Startup Disk created by Windows 95 is specific to the system on which you created it. This is due to the presence of the hidden file, DRVSPACE.BIN, which contains the index to the compressed files. If you use this disk on another computer, you may completely destroy the file system. To ensure that the compressed index is kept current, you need to re-create the Startup Disk as you add files and programs. If you want to create a generic Windows 95 boot disk that can be used on different Windows 95 computers, delete the DRVSPACE.BIN file by changing its attributes to –R –S –H and then using the DEL command.

Exam Essentials

The exam may cover any of the areas surveyed in this section. It will probably concentrate on the different files associated with the boot-up process and the sequence in which the system files are called on in the boot-up process.

Know the basic loading sequence of the boot-up files.   The MS-DOS boot sequence is IO.SYS, MSDOS.SYS, CONFIG.SYS, COMMAND.COM, and AUTOEXEC.BAT. The PC-DOS boot-up process is IBMBIO.COM, IBMDOS.COM, CONFIG.SYS, COMMAND.COM, and AUTOEXEC.BAT. The Windows 3.*x* boot order is KERNEL386.EXE, GDI.EXE, USER.EXE, and PROGMAN.EXE. Windows 95 boots up with IO.SYS, MSDOS .SYS, CONFIG.SYS, AUTOEXEC.BAT, VMM32.VxD, GDI.EXE/ GDI32.DLL, USER.EXE/USER32.DLL, and the desktop.

Be familiar with the different ways Windows 95 can be booted. Windows 95 can be booted into the Startup menu by pressing F8 at the "Loading Windows 95" message. The Startup menu provides the following ways in which Windows 95 can be booted: Normal, Logged, Safe Mode, Safe Mode with Networking, Step-by-Step Confirmation, Command Prompt Only, and Safe Mode Command Prompt. In addition, the Startup menu allows you to boot a previous version of an OS if you have upgraded and kept your original OS intact.

Key Terms and Concepts

ASCII text file: A file that contains ASCII characters that can be easily read with text editors or the DOS TYPE command.

Boot disk: A diskette that contains the system boot-up files. It is used to boot the computer when you need a generic boot-up sequence devoid of any drivers and TSRs, or when the hard drive is experiencing boot-up problems. See also *Emergency boot disk*.

Boot loader: The boot loader is a small utility program in BIOS that searches out and loads the master boot record, and starts the boot-up process for the OS.

Boot-up sequence: The sequential order in which the system files that make up the OS are loaded into memory.

Disk compression: The process of creating more space on a disk drive than would normally be available.

Emergency boot disk: A diskette that contains the boot-up files and the utilities needed to fix the more common hard drive problems.

Graphics engine: The part of the OS that controls and manages the graphics displays for the system.

Input engine: The component of the OS that controls and manages the input devices for the system.

Kernel: The essential, core portion of the operating system.

MS-DOS: The disk operating system created and marketed by Microsoft.

PC-DOS: The disk operating system created and marketed by IBM.

POST: The power on self test that the system is ROM-programmed to perform each time the system is cold booted. The POST routine checks out the system hardware and initiates the boot-loader utility.

Virtual Machine Manager: The component of Windows 95 that sets and manages the environments (virtual machines) that are created for each active application in the system. It also manages the virtual device drivers attached to all the I/O port addresses.

Sample Questions

1. What is the boot sequence of PC-DOS?

   A. IO.SYS, MSDOS.SYS, COMMAND.COM, AUTOEXEC.BAT

B. IO.SYS, MSDOS.SYS, CONFIG.SYS, COMMAND.COM

C. IBMBIO.SYS, IBMDOS.SYS, CONFIG.SYS, COMMAND .COM, AUTOEXEC.BAT

D. IBMBIO.COM, IBMDOS.COM, CONFIG.SYS, COMMAND .COM, AUTOEXEC.BAT

Answer: D. PC-DOS is the IBM DOS OS.

2. Which two files provide Windows 95 with its enhanced graphics and user-interface engines?

  A. GDI.EXE

  B. GDI32.DLL

  C. USER.EXE

  D. USER32.DLL

Answer: B, D. Windows 95 gets its enhanced interface abilities with the GDI32.DLL and USER32.DLL files.

Identify procedures for loading/adding device drivers and the necessary software for certain devices.

The purpose for this objective of the exam is to test your knowledge of loading and configuring device drivers and utilities on a computer system, which is a critical part of servicing and upgrading computer systems. Without an understanding of how to load drivers into your system, you will be severely limited in what you can do with your computer system.

Critical Information

Even though most hardware devices come with their own installation programs that fully automate the installation process, a few don't. In addition, you will come across some installation packages that have bugs in them and don't work. In these instances, knowing how to get the device drivers loaded is a must.

Loading Drivers and Utilities under DOS

Device-driver setup utilities must be run from the DOS prompt. The setup utility for the device will install the appropriate files on the hard disk and modify the CONFIG.SYS and AUTOEXEC.BAT files as needed.

In situations where the device or application does not have a setup utility, you will need to create a directory for the files on the hard disk, copy the files from the installation diskette to the new directory, and make appropriate changes to your CONFIG.SYS and AUTOEXEC.BAT files. In any case, you should have a set of directions describing what needs to be done.

NOTE It is becoming more common to have the installation routine in a self-extracting .EXE file. When run, this file will expand the compressed files that it contains. These expanded files are what you use to perform the installation. It usually is best to copy the self-extracting file into a temporary directory by itself before expanding it.

While most installation programs create backup copies of your CONFIG.SYS and AUTOEXEC.BAT files, some do not. Before performing the installation, make backup copies of these files. This will make it easier to restore your system to its original condition if the installation doesn't work right.

Loading Drivers and Utilities under Windows 3.*x*

Drivers and utilities for Windows 3.*x* are normally loaded through either the Setup utility or the Control Panel. Devices that come with their own installation disk can be installed with Start ➤ Run. You can also run these installation programs from the File Manager.

Keyboard, mouse, and monitor drivers are normally installed using the Setup utility. Printer drivers are normally installed through the Printers icon in the Control Panel. All other drivers are installed through the Drivers icon in the Control Panel.

Setup utilities will modify CONFIG.SYS, AUTOEXEC.BAT, WIN.INI, and SYSTEM.INI as needed. It is always a good idea to make a backup of your CONFIG.SYS, AUTOEXEC.BAT, WIN.INI, and SYSTEM.INI files before doing the installation. Some installation programs do not do this automatically, and trying to figure out what was changed in these files can be time consuming and labor intensive.

Windows 95 and Plug and Play (PnP)

Plug and Play is a new feature found in Windows 95, and is one of the features that has made Windows 95 so popular. Before the arrival of PnP, installing new hardware devices was a difficult and involved process that took time, patience, and determination. As more devices were added to the system, trying to juggle the system's IRQs, DMAs, I/O ports, and memory addresses became more difficult. Some devices seemed destined to be totally incompatible with the system and refused to mesh into the system's configuration without messing up other devices. PnP was designed to bring an end to the entire hassle associated with hardware installation and operating system upgrades.

PnP is a specification standard developed by Microsoft, Intel, and Phoenix Technologies. It involves the makeup of the system BIOS, the BIOS built into the hardware devices, and the operating system. Its major aim is to set up a two-way relationship between the OS and device so that the device is integrated into the system.

PnP relieves the user from the tedious task of configuring those pesky IRQ and DMA settings. On laptops, PnP takes over the task of linking the laptop to a standard computer, and assists in resetting and matching the system resources for any docking stations to which you connect it.

Basic Components of PnP

There are seven major components of the PnP system: the system BIOS, the hardware device BIOS, the Registry, the hardware tree, the INF files, the application programming interfaces (APIs), and the PnP or Configuration Manager.

System ROM BIOS: Designed with an element that searches for, identifies, and attaches the PnP-designed devices to the system.

Device BIOS: Designed to contain a means of identifying itself to the PnP BIOS.

Hardware tree: The database containing information on the devices in the system and their configurations. The hardware tree is built by the Configuration Manager and stored in memory each time the system boots.

INF files: Contain information about particular devices and are used to initialize the device to the system.

API files: Sometimes called events, these files are program interfaces that contain protocols determining what an application can do. They are also used to report changes in the system's configuration.

Configuration Manager: The heart of the PnP system. Once the PnP components and other devices have been properly identified, the Configuration Manager allocates the necessary resources required by the devices.

Registry: A centralized database used in Windows 95 that contains all the settings for the system. In its PnP role, the Registry allows the PnP manager to access the hardware specifications that it contains.

The actual operations associated with the PnP processes are totally transparent to the user. The user does not have any direct method of intervention in the process.

PnP in Operations

As the system boots, the PnP portion of the system ROM BIOS searches out the PnP devices attached to the system. It then identifies their device type and name (usually the manufacturer's model number). When queried, the PnP BIOS of the device responds to the system BIOS by giving the system BIOS the information it needs to identify it by type, category, and name.

The OS verifies the device's category as being PnP, then uses the rest of the information to search the Registry for the type of device (e.g., hard disk drive) and its name (e.g., manufacturer and model number). It then uses the information it locates in the Registry to assign the proper IRQ, DMA, I/O, and such ports to the device.

All hardware configuration settings are assigned at the software level each time the computer is booted. There are four different ways to activate PnP:

Installation: During installation, you are prompted whether you want the installation utility to detect your hardware. If you indicate that you do, PnP is used to search for and set up your system's hardware components.

Add New Hardware: When you select the Add New Hardware icon in the Control Panel, you activate the Add New Hardware Wizard, which prompts you for whether you want detection done automatically. If you answer Yes, the Wizard uses PnP to locate, identify, and set up the new hardware.

Normal system boot: During the normal boot-up process, PnP actively seeks out new devices on the system. As the OS builds the Registry from the USER.DAT and SYSTEM.DAT files, PnP automatically assigns the appropriate resources to the devices in the Registry. If new PnP devices are located, it automatically sets them up and adds them to the Registry. If the device is not a PnP device, the system reports that it has found a new device and suggests you use the Add New Hardware Wizard to set it up.

Docking laptops: PnP is also activated when you place a portable computer such as a laptop into its docking station. With PnP, a portable computer can be inserted into its station using either a *warm docking* or a *hot docking* procedure.

- **Warm docking:** The insertion of the portable computer into its docking station while the computer is in its suspended sleep state with minimum power applied.

- **Hot docking:** The insertion of the portable computer into its docking station while the computer is fully powered.

- **Cold docking:** The insertion of a portable computer into its docking station when the power is off. PnP is not activated until the system is turned on.

What to Expect When Everything Works

When everything is loaded correctly, when all your system devices are PnP compatible, and when you have not overloaded your system, everything should work fine.

Since PnP operations are totally transparent to the user, you should not see anything about PnP at all. The system should function without any IRQ or DMA conflicts. Your mouse and your modem should be able to work at the same time. On a modern machine, your CD player should be able to play music while you are playing a full-screen version of *DOOM* without jerky sounds and images spoiling your session.

What to Expect When Something Goes Wrong

Since this is an imperfect world, problems can be expected to develop. Most problems that develop with PnP can be traced to the following causes:

- PnP is still a developing standard with some bugs that need to be worked out.

- Not all PnP devices are manufactured to the complete PnP standards.

- Device drivers may contain bugs.

- People are still attached to older, non-PnP hardware.

- System files can be lost or corrupted.

- The device itself may be broken.

A malfunction in the PnP feature can cause many diverse symptoms, depending on the problem and how it affects the system.

- If the Registry is corrupted, the system may not boot, or you may not have all your devices loaded during the boot-up process.

- If a device is not PnP compatible, is not working, or has a bug in its driver, the system may not be able to load the device, or if it does load it, the device may act weird.

There are just too many possible symptoms involved to cover them all. Basically, if you are having problems with a single device, it probably has something to do with the device. If you are experiencing problems with all of your devices, start to suspect the PnP component, the Registry, or the motherboard.

Loading Drivers and Utilities under Windows 95

Drivers are loaded into Windows 95 through the Add New Hardware icon in the Control Panel. The process is controlled by the Add New Hardware Wizard, which will offer you two options:

- The automated process is the default and causes the Wizard to search your system for the new hardware. This is the best way. Once Windows detects the device, it installs it into the system.

- With the manual process, you select the device type (CD-ROM, video driver, etc.) and the manufacturer and model number. You are also given a choice to use the installation disk that came with the device. This method should be used only if the Wizard cannot find your device. Entering the data in this manner does not integrate the device into the system.

NOTE   Many of the installation packages for device drivers do not come in a format recognized by the Wizard. In these cases, you may have to either use Start ➤ Run or run the utility from the DOS prompt. Make sure your system is backed up, especially the USER.DAT and SYSTEM.DAT files. It is also a good idea to back up the CONFIG.SYS, AUTOEXEC.BAT, WIN.INI, and SYSTEM.INI files as well.

Necessary Procedures

There are numerous ways to install device drivers into a Windows-based system. The ones described here are the most common and the most likely to be covered on the exam.

Installing Drivers in DOS

Drivers can be installed by the applications that require them or manually by a knowledgeable person.

Using the installation disk(s):

1. Back up the CONFIG.SYS and AUTOEXEC.BAT files.

2. Insert the installation disk and run the utility.

3. Verify the success of the installation by using the device.

Installing manually:

1. Back up the AUTOEXEC.BAT and CONFIG.SYS files.

2. Create a directory for the driver files and copy them into the new directory.

3. Add the appropriate DEVICE= command(s) to the CONFIG.SYS file.

4. Add any needed command lines to the AUTOEXEC.BAT file.

Installing Drivers in Windows 3.x with the Setup Utility

The Setup utility is probably the best way to install drivers into a Windows 3.x system because it performs most of the operations automatically using either the ones provided by Microsoft or the ones on the installation disk provided by the manufacturer.

1. Open the Main group window and double-click the Setup icon.

2. Click Options on the menu bar.

3. Select the Change System Settings option.

4. Click the box next to the type of hardware you want to install.

5. Click the brand name. If the brand name is not there, click Other and use the installation disk that came with the device.

Installing Drivers in Windows 3.x through the Control Panel

This procedure is a little more complicated than using the Setup utility. Basically, the results are the same whichever method you choose.

1. Open the Main group and double-click the Control Panel icon.

2. Double-click the Drivers icon. This will display the list of available drivers, as shown below.

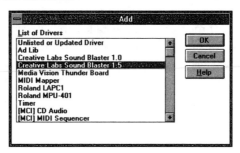

3. Click the Add button.

4. Click the manufacturer brand name for the device. If it is not listed, click the Unlisted/Updated Driver option and install the driver using the installation disk that came with the device.

Installing Drivers in Windows 95

Driver installation is almost a breeze with Windows 95. The Add New Hardware Wizard handles most of the process for you.

1. Double-click the Add New Hardware icon in the Control Panel.

2. Click the Next button to continue with installation. This will display a screen (shown below) prompting you for the type of installation you wish to perform.

3. Select the method of installation. Selecting Yes (Recommended) activates an automated search feature that will locate and install the device. Selecting No will start the process of describing the device to the system. This method does not install the device—it creates a file that will be used to add it to the system the next time the computer is booted.

4. To terminate the Wizard, click the Finish button when it appears.

Exam Essentials

This objective of the exam concentrates on testing your knowledge of hardware installation and the use of the drivers and installation utilities that come with the hardware device.

Be familiar with the procedures involved in installing device drivers under DOS. Device drivers can be installed in DOS either manually or by using the installation disk(s) that came with the device.

Be familiar with the procedures for installing device drivers under Windows 3.*x*. The Setup utility and the Control Panel are the two major methods used to install drivers in Windows 3.*x*. The keyboard, monitor, and mouse are installed using the Setup utility. Printers and other devices must use the Control Panel.

Be familiar with the procedures for installing device drivers under Windows 95. Device drivers are loaded into Windows 95 using the Add New Hardware icon in the Control Panel. Double-clicking the icon will launch the Add New Hardware Wizard. Having the system search for the device is recommended since the system will locate and integrate the device into itself. If you supply the setup information manually, it creates a file that may or may not be operational. You won't know if you have a successful installation until the system is rebooted and the device activated.

Be familiar with the purpose of PnP. The purpose of Plug and Play (PnP) is to relieve the user from the frustrating tasks associated with the installation of new hardware. It is designed to be a totally transparent process that configures all of the system's hardware without user involvement.

Know the major components of the PnP system. The major components of the PnP system include the ROM BIOS of the computer, the BIOS on the device, the OS PnP manager, and the Registry.

Be familiar with the ways that PnP is activated. PnP is activated through the installation utility, the normal boot-up process, and the Add New Hardware Wizard. It is also activated when you perform a warm or hot docking with a portable computer.

Know what to expect when PnP is working properly. When PnP is working, you will notice nothing but a properly functioning system. PnP is totally transparent to the user and will take care of all hardware settings itself. When PnP is not working correctly, you will experience some sort of problems with your hardware.

Key Terms and Concepts

Device driver: A program that facilitates communication between a piece of hardware, such as a printer, and the computer system. A driver will initialize the device to the system and provide the full range of features to the OS.

DMA (direct memory access): A DMA is a direct channel into RAM memory. It is used by devices such as the hard drive to access memory addresses without the help of the CPU. It speeds up operations.

Docking: Placing a portable computer into its docking station.

I/O (input/output) ports: Memory addresses assigned to a device that allow it to receive and transmit information.

Installation Utility or Program: A small program that is used to install drivers into the system.

IRQ (Interrupt ReQuest): The means by which a device signals the CPU, informing it that the device has something that needs processing.

Loading: Installing the driver into the system configuration and memory.

Memory address: A location in physical memory that is given a numeric value for identification purposes.

Plug and Play (PnP): A feature of Windows 95 that allows the system to automatically locate and configure system devices.

Registry: A centralized database containing the system configuration settings.

ROM BIOS: A chip on the motherboard that contains programs for checking out the system and starting the loading process for the OS.

Setup utility: The installation program used in Windows.

Transparent: When things are transparent to the user, the user does not see them and is relieved of any tasks associated with them.

Sample Questions

1. Keyboard drivers are installed in Windows 95 through the Control Panel. True or false?

   Answer: False. Keyboards, monitors, and mice are installed through SETUP.

2. Key files such as CONFIG.SYS and AUTOEXEC.BAT should be _____ before starting any installation procedure.

   Answer: backed up. Key files that will be modified during the installation should be backed up to facilitate restoring the system in case the installation fails.

3. In what ways can PnP be activated?

   A. Installation

   B. Normal boot up

   C. Add New Hardware Wizard

   D. Docking a portable

   Answer: A, B, C, D. PnP is activated by all of the mentioned methods.

4. The Registry is a part of the PnP operation. True or false?

   Answer: True. The Registry is consulted by PnP to determine the identification of installed devices so that it can assign the appropriate resources.

Identify the procedures for changing options, configuring, and using the Windows printing subsystem.

The objectives in this portion of the exam will explore your knowledge of the printing services provided by Windows 3.x and Windows 95. A large share of user problems is associated with not being able to get the printer to work properly. Knowing how Windows activates and controls the printing process is essential for a service technician.

Critical Information

Printing is one of the most important features of a computer system. It is essential to business and individuals who wish to communicate with others. Besides the monitor, printers are the most widely used output device.

Many users have complex systems that have several computers connected to them or are using shared printers through either a network or a shared printer interface device. Configurations for user printer configurations abound—so do the problems associated with them. To diagnose and resolve printer problems efficiently and effectively, you need an extensive knowledge of how the components work with each other and how the operating system accepts and uses the configuration information that is supplied to it. As a service technician, you will spend a good deal of your time installing printers and upgrading their device drivers.

The Windows 3.x Printing Subsystem

Installing printer drivers is a simple matter under Windows 3.x. All you need to do is use the Printers option in the Control Panel and either install one of the drivers listed in the Printers list or use the driver disk that came with your printer. After you have installed the driver, you need to connect the printer to an LPT or COM port, and set the configuration parameters for the printer.

NOTE   Printers and their drivers are installed through the Printers option in the Control Panel. The actual printing is controlled by the Print Manager, which allows you to start, stop, pause, and delete print jobs in the print queue.

Once the drivers have been installed, don't forget to set the menu options on the printer. This is usually accomplished by using the printer's onboard menu facility. Consult the printer manual for the details on configuring the printer.

The Windows 95 Printing Subsystem

To install printer drivers in Windows 95, you use the Printer Wizard, which is activated through the Printers icon found in either Start ➤ Settings or the My Computer icon on the desktop.

Necessary Procedures

The procedures for installing printers in Windows 3.*x* or Windows 95 are a part of the exam. A basic outline of these procedures is provided below.

SEE ALSO   For a more in-depth explanation of the procedures involved in installing printers, please consult another source such as David Groth's *A+: Windows/DOS Study Guide* published by Sybex.

Setting Up a Printer under Windows 3.x

Installing and setting up a printer in the Windows 3.x environment involves the use of the Windows Printers list or the installation diskette that came with the printer.

1. Open the Main group window and double-click the Control Panel.

2. Double-click the Printers icon. This will display a screen showing the manufacturers and model numbers for the printer drivers built into Windows 3.x (shown below).

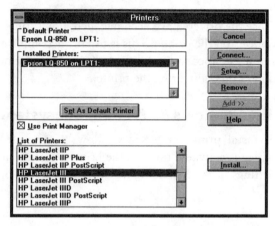

3. Select the printer from the Printers list. If it is not listed, read the user manual for a printer that it can emulate. If one is not mentioned, use the installation disk that came with the printer. If a disk was not provided, call the manufacturer for a driver or information on which printer it can emulate.

4. Set the printer's resolution, paper orientation, and paper source.

5. Connect the printer to an LPT (parallel) or COM (serial) port and set the time-out features.

6. If there is more than one printer, set which one you want to be the default printer.

Setting Up a Printer under Windows 95

Printer installation under Windows 95 is a bit easier than under Windows 3.*x* due to the improved GUI and the Add Printer Wizard that walks you through the process.

1. Open My Computer and double-click the Printers icon, or choose Start ➤ Settings ➤ Printers. Either of these actions will display the contents of the Printers folder, as shown below.

2. Double-click the Add Printer icon to activate the Add Printer Wizard.

3. Click the Next button on the welcome screen.

4. Select Local Printer for a single, stand-alone, non-networked printer. Select Network Printer if the printer will be a network resource. After you have made your choice, click Next. This will display the Manufacturers/Printers screen, as shown below.

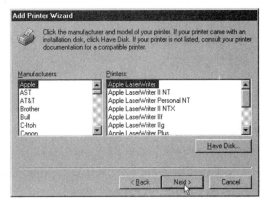

5. Select the manufacturer that made the printer and then select the model number of the printer. If the printer is not listed, use the disk that came with the printer. When you have finished with the manufacturer and model number, click Next.

TIP Avoid using Windows 3.*x* drivers. These drivers are written for a 16-bit system and cannot take advantage of the full features of a 32-bit system.

---

6. Select the port you wish the printer connected to, and configure the port as to DOS spooling and check-port features. Click Next to proceed.

   - Spool MS-DOS Print Jobs is selected by default. It allows DOS applications to spool their documents to a print queue before printing, thus freeing up the CPU for other tasks as the document prints.

   - Check Quick Port State Before Printing forces the system to check the status of the printer connection before sending any information to the printer.

7. Accept the name of the printer or rename it in the dialog box displayed on the screen.

8. If this is the default printer, click the Yes box to indicate that it is the default printer for the system.

9. Print a test page to check on the success of the installation.

10. Click the Finish button to complete installation.

Exam Essentials

The exam will test your knowledge of what procedures to follow in the installation of printer drivers. To do this, it will ask specific questions concerning the location of the folders and icons needed to install and set up the driver.

Know the basic methodology for installing print drivers. The basic process for installing device drivers is to install the driver through an installation routine such as Windows Control Panel or the installation disk that came with the printer; configure the printer to your system needs; connect the printer to the appropriate port; and set the printer as the primary default printer.

Know the location of the Printers icon. In Windows 3.*x*, the Printers icon is located in the Control Panel. In Windows 95, the Printers icon is located in the My Computer icon or under Start ➢ Settings.

Be familiar with the installation process for loading a printer device driver in Windows 3.*x*. Loading the printer drivers requires the Printers option under the Control Panel. You select the manufacturer and model number from the Printers list or use an OEM disk provided by the manufacturer.

Be familiar with the installation of a printer driver in Windows 95. Windows 95 uses the Add Printer Wizard to install the printer drivers. The Wizard is activated through either the My Computer icon or Start ➢ Settings. You will probably need the Windows 95 installation disks or CD-ROM to install the device.

Key Terms and Concepts

Fast printing: The capability for the print job to be sent directly to the printer.

Paper orientation: Paper orientation refers to the way the printer views how the paper is aligned in the printer. Portrait refers to the vertical positioning of the paper (8.5×11), and landscape refers to the horizontal alignment (11×8.5).

Print quality: Print quality refers to the high-resolution factor that makes the font appear as close to typewriter-perfect characters as possible.

Resolution: Resolution for a printer refers to how many dots are placed within an inch of print space. The higher the resolution, the closer the printing gets to reaching near-letter quality (NLQ)—higher yet, it approaches letter quality (LQ). Lower resolutions are used for draft-quality documents.

Time-outs: Periods of time used to delay some action from the printer before it acts according to its program. If the paper runs out in a printer, you would like to know it. However, if the printer is across the room and you want to change paper types, you do not want the computer to disconnect your connection while you are making the switch. In this case, the printer time-outs would be lengthened to allow you the extra time needed to change the paper before the printer disconnects.

Sample Questions

1. A Windows 3.1 printer device driver is normally installed through the _____.

   A. Print Manager

   B. Device Manager

   C. Control Panel

   D. My Computer

   Answer: C. Printer drivers are installed through the Printers icon located in the Control Panel.

2. To load a printer driver in Windows 95, you start by launching the Add Printer Wizard with the Add Printer icon. Where is this icon located?

   A. Printers folder

   B. Settings menu

   C. My Computer

   D. Control Panel folder

   Answer: A. The Add Printer icon is located in the Printers folder, which can be accessed through either the Control Panel or the Printers folder in My Computer.

Identify the procedures for installing and launching typical Windows and non-Windows applications.

This section of the exam focuses on your knowledge of the procedures used to install and run programs.

Critical Information

Installing software is one of the major tasks of using a computer. Users constantly add new programs and upgrade older programs. Much of the information that is found in the application's user guide is worthless. Knowing the basic concepts and procedures for installing software packages is a very important element to add to your skills as a service technician. With a basic understanding of software installation, you can install the vast majority of the more modern applications being produced today.

All applications consist of a file or group of files that reside in a directory on your storage media. Program files are binary executable files. This means that the files are compiled machine-code files (not ASCII) that can be used as commands that the OS will recognize. For instance, WIN.COM is a binary executable file used to launch Windows. Typing **WIN** at the DOS prompt will launch (or run) Windows.

NOTE Executable files contain instructions that tell the computer what to do and how to do it. There are three types of executable files, with file extensions of COM, EXE, or BAT. COM files are binary executable files, which are usually very small program files or utilities. EXE files are binary executable files, which are usually larger application files. BAT files are ASCII executable files that consist of DOS commands that are executed as one large batch of commands.

It is always a good idea to make a backup of CONFIG.SYS, AUTOEXEC.BAT, WIN.INI, and SYSTEM.INI along with the entire WINDOWS and WINDOWS\SYSTEM directories. New programs will copy files into the directories, and many times they will overwrite files that are already there.

To execute a program, you must use the entire path name for the file or make sure that the file's directory is part of the system's search path.

Installing and Launching Applications under Windows 3.*x*

Loading any software designed for Windows 3.*x* is a simple and identical process due to the uniformity of the common-user-interface design of Windows. Most Windows-based programs require you to use the Windows environment for the installation. The installation utility (usually named SETUP.EXE or INSTALL.EXE) can be run from File ➤ Run or by using the File Manager. Most applications will install themselves into their own directory and create their own program group. Once the application has been installed, you may need to tweak the configuration to your tastes.

Launching a program is a Windows term that means to call the program into active memory. It is another way of saying that you are running or executing the program. The Windows GUI facilitates the launching process by using icons to identify the program. To launch a program, all that is needed is to open the appropriate program group and double-click the program's icon. The hardest part of launching an application under Windows is remembering which program group it is in.

You can also associate an application to a particular file extension. Double-clicking a document will launch the application associated with the file extension on the document and load the document into the application.

DOS-based applications are 16-bit programs, are resource intensive, and do not have the control features built into them as do the 32-bit applications. For most of them to function at their best within Windows 95, they must be tailored to the system. System variables must be set to adjust to the demands of the program. This is accomplished through the PIF Editor, which creates the necessary information that will allow the OS to adjust system variables to meet the application's demands. Once an application PIF file has been created, the program is launched using the PIF.

DOS programs are resource intensive and place a tremendous demand on system resources. The PIF Editor is used to change the default settings used for the majority of programs to what the application actually needs. If a DOS-based program is giving you problems, create a PIF file for it or modify the PIF that is used to launch it. To check the parameters needed by the application, check the application's documentation or call its technical-support desk. Many times it will require experimentation and testing to determine the necessary settings.

Installing and Launching Applications under Windows 95

Installing software packages into a Windows 95 system is just as easy as it is in Windows 3.*x*. With Windows 95, you can install the application from Start ➤ Run, by using Explorer to launch the installation utility, or by using the Add/Remove Programs Wizard (Figure 3.2) found in the Control Panel.

FIGURE 3.2: Add/Remove Programs Wizard

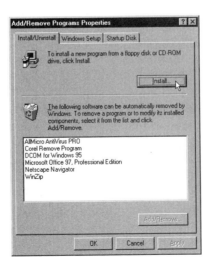

If you may need to uninstall the application at a later date, you should use the Add New Program Wizard to do so. Using the Wizard sets up a file-identification process that keeps track of all the files that are installed. When it is time to remove the program, the OS simply uses this file to delete everything that was loading. Deleting an application by hand will still leave DLL and other files that you cannot relate to the program.

Launching a program with Windows 95 is a bit simpler than with Windows 3.*x*. Most of the clicking process has been reduced. The most common way to launch a program is to double-click a document file. This will load the application that created it and load the document into the application. You can also launch an application by highlighting the Programs option on the Start menu. This will display a list of installed applications. A single-click on any of the programs listed will activate the program. A third method for launching programs is to use Explorer to locate the program file and double-click it.

DOS-based applications are 16-bit programs, are resource intensive, and do not have the control features built into them as do the 32-bit applications. For most of them to function at their best within Windows 95, they must be tailored to the system. System variables must be set to adjust to the demands of the program. This is accomplished through the PIF Editor, which creates the necessary information that will allow the OS to adjust system variables to meet the application's demands. Once an application PIF file has been created, the program is launched using the PIF. These programs will usually require entries in the CONFIG.SYS file.

Windows 3.*x* applications are also 16-bit programs and will usually require entries in the WIN.INI and SYSTEM.INI files before they will function properly. These entries are usually provided during the application's installation.

Exam Essentials

The essential elements covered in the exam will concentrate on the tools and procedures used for installing applications.

Be familiar with all the methods for installing applications in Windows 3.x. You can install applications in Windows 3.*x* by using the application's installation utility, which can be activated through either the File Manager or File ➤ Run in the Program Manager. DOS programs require you to create a PIF file that will set the Windows environment to the needs of the application.

Be familiar with the methods used to install applications in Windows 95. The recommended way to install programs in Windows 95 is to use the Add/Remove Programs utility in the Control Panel. You can also use Windows Explorer or Start ➤ Run.

Key Terms and Concepts

16-bit applications: Applications that are created with 16-bit code. These programs were designed for DOS and Windows 3.*x*.

32-bit applications: Applications that are created with 32-bit code. They have more control features built into them and are designed for Windows 95 and Windows NT.

Associate: The process of linking an application to a document. By activating the document, the OS will automatically launch the program first and then load the document into the program.

Binary file: A file that consists of binary data. These files can be data files or executable files.

Executable file: A file that can be run by typing its filename at the DOS prompt.

File: A collection of information on storage media. The two basic types of files are data files and program files. Data files contain data or documents created by an application; program files are executable and contain a set of instructions that tells the computer which tasks to perform.

File Manager: The Windows 3.*x* utility that is used to manage files.

Launch: To initiate the process of loading an application into memory. It is synonymous with running and executing a program.

Load: To initiate the process that places either data or an application into memory.

PIF (program information file):   A special binary file used by Windows to configure system resources to DOS-based during the initial stages of launching the program.

PIF Editor: A utility used to create program information files (PIFs).

Windows Explorer: The Windows 95 utility that replaced the Windows 3.x File Manager. It is used to manage the Windows 95 file structure.

Sample Questions

1. What is a PIF file?

   A. An ASCII text file containing information about a program

   B. A binary executable file used to execute a program

   C. An ASCII executable file used by Windows to run a program

   D. A special file used by Windows to launch a program

   Answer: D. A PIF (program information file) is a special file containing setup information that adjusts the system to the needs of the DOS program.

2. What is the best way to install a program into a Windows 95 system?

   A. Through the Windows Explorer

   B. Through the program's installation utility

   C. Through the Start ➤ Run option

   D. Through the Add/Remove Programs icon in the Control Panel

   Answer: D. The Add/Remove Programs utility will keep a record of the files that were installed. When you need to get rid of the program, you can easily remove it and all the files associated with it.

CHAPTER

4

Diagnosing and
Troubleshooting

A+ Exam Objectives Covered in This Chapter:

▶ Recognize and interpret the meaning of common error codes and start-up messages from the boot sequence, and identify steps to correct the problems. *(pages 169 – 176)*

▶ Recognize Windows-specific printing problems, and identify the procedures for correcting them. *(pages 176 – 184)*

▶ Recognize common problems and determine how to resolve them. *(pages 185 – 206)*

▶ Identify concepts relating to viruses and virus types—their danger, their symptoms, sources of viruses, how they infect, how to protect against them, and how to identify and remove them. *(pages 207 – 219)*

The major focuses of this domain are troubleshooting and diagnosing common problems encountered on a PC. In particular, this domain concentrates on the error codes and messages that the OS displays, and the procedures needed to resolve the problems that caused them.

The major purpose of this domain of the examination is to test your knowledge about the concepts, procedures, and tools you can use to determine and resolve computer problems associated with the OS and application software.

NOTE This domain comprises 25 percent of the exam. Troubleshooting and diagnosing computer problems are the crux of a service technician's existence. Mastering the objectives in this domain is essential for passing the exam.

The service technician's ability to troubleshoot, diagnose, and resolve system problems in an effective and efficient manner is the measure of their expertise. With this in mind, let's explore some of the fundamental concepts associated with troubleshooting and diagnosing computer system problems.

Operational problems in a microcomputer system occur in any of four major areas:

Operator error: Operator errors are a result of insufficient training. The user deletes or modifies files or system variables that should not be changed.

System environment: System environment problems occur when one of the system files has been corrupted or improperly modified. Improper entries for system commands and variables can also cause this type of problem.

Hardware: Hardware problems occur when device drivers are not set up correctly, the device itself has not been configured to system requirements, or the hardware itself just is not working.

Software: Software problems can occur when the application is installed incorrectly, files become corrupted, the user has used the wrong settings, or the software itself is full of bad code and was not thoroughly tested.

The majority of system problems are the result of corrupted or missing files. *Corrupted files* are usually caused by power fluctuations that destroy critical files that are open at the time—by sudden discharges of static electricity as a file is being saved, or by EMI/RFI interference from flourescent lights or electric motors that are too close to cable runs. *Missing files* are usually caused by untrained users who unintentionally delete them (e.g., using DEL*.* in the C: drive when the user thinks they are in the A: drive), or by power users trying to tweak their system.

Diagnosing problems in the operating system and application software requires logical and deductive reasoning. You must follow a step-by-step approach to the problem. The process involves six basic concepts:

1. Focus on what is applicable to the problem. If the problem seems to be printer related, you don't need to check out the video or sound drivers. Don't get sidetracked.

2. Probe the situation. Ask questions of the user that will narrow the problem down and isolate it.

3. Analyze the data you have received and determine possible causes.

4. Try to re-create the problem. By duplicating the problem, you can analyze the problem itself and not the circumstantial symptoms of the problem.

5. Resolve the problem, which can take the forms of swapping out devices with working systems, installing new drivers, and modifying system files.

6. Document the steps you take to resolve the problem. This makes it easier to take up from where you left off, and will create a database of potential problems and their solutions.

If you have to make changes to the system files, do so one change at a time. Make the change, then test it. If it doesn't work, try another one and test it.

Most software problems can be fixed by making changes to the CONFIG.SYS file or the application's options/preferences. You may need to contact the software vendor for additional software code—called *patches*, *upgrades*, or *service paks*—to resolve the problem. At times, you may have to reinstall the application; at other times, you may have to reinstall the operating system. This is where a current backup of a working system comes in handy.

The fastest way of determining whether a problem is software or hardware related is to boot the system with a generic boot disk. The boot disk should contain the basic operating system files. If the system boots and you can use the suspected hardware device, the problem is in the software arena. Do not use the defective system's system files since these may be the cause of the problem.

The boot disk should also have a diagnostic program, an antivirus program, and a copy of SCANDISK, FDISK, SYS, and FORMAT. These tools will allow you to fix the more common computer problems.

Recognize and interpret the meaning of common error codes and start-up messages from the boot sequence, and identify steps to correct the problems.

This objective concentrates on the errors associated with the boot sequence. A firm grasp of the objectives in this section will help you diagnose and resolve system problems.

Critical Information

Troubleshooting and diagnosing system problems are the essential parts of a service technician's career. Many times the problem is associated with the boot process. Knowing the more common error messages and what they mean will improve your ability to rapidly determine what is wrong with a system.

Common Boot Problems in DOS

DOS has two distinct ways to inform you that it is experiencing a problem: beep codes and error messages.

Beep codes are provided by the system's ROM BIOS and are part of the POST. For most IBM-compatible PCs, these codes are as follows:

- One beep followed by three, four, or five beeps usually means you have a bad motherboard.

- Two beeps should be supplemented by an error code on the screen.

- Two beeps followed by three, four, or five beeps indicate there is a problem with the first 64KB of RAM.

- Three beeps followed by three, four, or five beeps are usually associated with either a bad keyboard controller or a bad video controller card.

- Four beeps followed by two, three, or four beeps indicate there is a problem with the serial or parallel port, or that the system timer is gone.

NOTE Beep codes are BIOS specific. The codes listed here are what you will find on most machines, but there will be differences.

Boot-up *error messages* are also provided by the system BIOS. The more common boot-up problems and their error messages include:

Device *xxxx* Not Found: This error message means that a device driver in CONFIG.SYS could not be located. Take note of the device name (*xxxx*) and try to locate it. If it is not present, copy it from a working system.

Error Codes: On some systems, the POST will generate error codes instead of (or along with) error messages. The most frequently encountered codes can be broken down into the following series:

100	Motherboard problems
200	Memory RAM problems
300	Keyboard problems
700	Coprocessor problems
900	Parallel port problems
1700	Hard disk drive or disk controller problems
6000	SCSI device or network problems

Error in CONFIG.SYS Line *nnnn*: This message indicates that a command line (number *nnnn*) in CONFIG.SYS is not written correctly. Check out the line number and rewrite the command line correctly.

File Not Found: During boot up, this error message means that a command line in the AUTOEXEC.BAT file has been written incorrectly. Check AUTOEXEC.BAT and rewrite the command line.

Fixed Disk Error: This message could mean that the hard drive is corrupted or broken. Usually it signifies a hardware problem and requires you to replace the hard drive. You can try to fix it by performing a FDISK /MBR to restore the master boot record and a SYS C: to replace the operating system. If those attempts fail to fix the problem, you can try to repartition and reformat the drive.

Operating System Not Found: This indicates that the OS files are corrupted or that the primary drive does not have a partition set as the active partition. Use FDISK to view the partition table. If there is no active partition, set the primary DOS partition as the active partition. If the drive has an active partition, use the SYS C: command to restore the system files to the drive. If neither of these attempts work, you will have to repartition and reformat the drive.

System Hangs or Locks Up: This situation happens too frequently. Many different things can cause this type of problem. The most common cause is a corrupted master boot record or a conflict in device drivers being loaded by CONFIG.SYS. Boot the system with a boot diskette and try to access the C: drive. If you can get into the drive, REM out all the command lines in both CONFIG.SYS and AUTOEXEC.BAT and then try to reboot the system. If the system boots, the problem is in the system files; if it doesn't, the problem is in the master boot record or with the hidden OS files. Try FDISK /MBR and SYS C: to fix these problems. If these don't work, repartition and reformat the drive.

Common Boot Problems in Windows 3.*x*

Windows 3.*x* has a lot of different problems that can be associated with the boot-up process. The majority of problems will involve improperly configured device drivers, corrupted files, or lack of memory. You may see the following error messages during boot up:

Application Execution Error: A corrupted Windows file causes this error message. You will have to reinstall this Windows file to fix it. Sometimes, finding the specific file needed is difficult. As a result, from time to time, reinstalling Windows will resolve the problem. The trouble with this approach is that you haven't identified what the exact problem is—if it resurfaces, where does that leave you? Many times, it is the application you installed—you need to uninstall that application, contact the vendor for specific help, and proceed from that point.

General Protection Fault: During boot up, this error usually indicates a corrupted file. You should back up your drive and reinstall Windows. You may also have a corrupted or defective disk. Run SCANDISK to fix this problem.

Insufficient Disk Space: This error message indicates that your available hard disk space is not enough for Windows' swap file.

Insufficient Memory: This error message indicates there is not enough RAM installed to load all the device drivers, TSRs, fonts, and wallpaper you have chosen to load into memory. If you are tight on RAM, eliminate the wallpaper, remove most of the fonts (WIN.INI), and do away with your TSRs. You can also install more memory.

Common Boot Problems in Windows 95

Many things can go wrong with Windows 95 during the boot-up process. Most of the problems encountered during boot up are caused by corrupted or missing device drivers, a corrupted hard drive, a corrupted Registry, or a Win16 driver that has reached past the virtual device driver assigned to look after it. Some of the more common error messages you will encounter during the Windows 95 boot sequence include:

Boot Partition Error: This problem is caused by a corrupted disk compression utility/file, a network drive mapped over the primary drive, or a corrupted partition table. Use the DRVSPACE utilities to recover from a compressed disk problem. Insure that the network drives are properly mapped, and use SCANDISK, FDISK/MBR, and SYS C: to fix the partition table. If these methods fail to work, you will need to repartition, reformat, and reinstall the OS.

Corrupted Registry: When the Registry file gets scrambled by an unknown source, it causes this problem. To fix the Registry, you must replace the SYSTEM.DAT and USER.DAT files with their backup counterparts—SYSTEM.DA0 and USER.DA0—and reboot the system.

Safe Mode: This screen is presented when the Registry has a problem. If you turn off the system without going through the shutdown procedure, it usually causes Windows 95 to boot into Safe mode. In this mode, only the default drivers and the bare essentials of the OS are loaded. It allows the Registry and other system functions to recover from the improper shutdown.

System Locks Up during Boot Up: An errant Win16 driver or TSR usually causes this problem. Boot the system into DOS mode and launch Windows 95 by typing **WIN /B** at the command prompt. This will create the BOOTLOG.TXT file. The OS will then write every system event to this file. By examining this file, you can determine which driver or TSR is causing the problem. See Figure 4.1 for a sample BOOTLOG.TXT file.

Exam Essentials

The exam will test your understanding of the more common error codes that could occur during the boot-up process. You will have to be able to determine their most probable causes and provide solutions for them.

Know the common error codes and messages that you can expect to encounter during the boot-up process. The errors associated with DOS fall into three major areas: a corrupted boot record, a corrupted file in the OS, or a bad or missing device driver. Errors associated with Windows 3.x fall into two major categories: corrupted system files or insufficient resources (especially memory and available hard disk space). In Windows 95, the errors can be grouped into three categories: bad partition record, corrupted Registry, or bad device drivers.

FIGURE 4.1: Sample contents of the BOOTLOG.TXT file

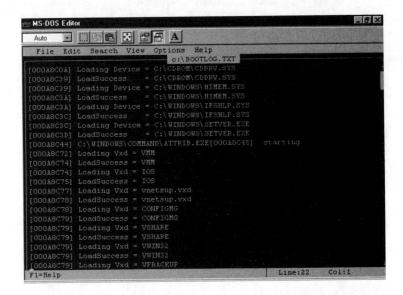

Be familiar with the most common solutions used to fix boot-up problems. Boot-up problems in DOS are usually fixed by using FDISK /MBR or SYS C: to fix the master boot record and corrupted system files. In Windows 3.*x* and 95, you can use the WIN /B command to create a boot log that records each action the OS takes during boot up, which you can then use to determine the driver or file that needs replacing. SCAN-DISK is also used to fix problems with the boot record.

Know the process of restoring the Windows Registry. Windows 95 keeps backup copies of the USER.DAT and SYSTEM.DAT files that it uses to create the Registry. These files are USER.DA0 and SYSTEM.DA0. To restore the Registry, copy the backup files over the .DAT files, or delete the originals and rename the .DA0 files to .DAT.

Key Terms and Concepts

Application error: A problem generated by a malfunction in an application. Corrupt files, improper settings, or insufficient resources are common causes of application errors.

Beep codes: A pattern of beeps built into the ROM BIOS. These beep codes will help diagnose the type of any system problem by using the PC's speakers to sound a series of tones.

Boot errors: Problems the system experiences during the boot-up process. Common causes of boot errors are corrupted system files, a corrupted partition table, a corrupted FAT, or a bad disk drive.

Boot partition errors: Problems associated with the master boot record. Common causes include a corrupt partition table, a corrupt network mapping setting, or a lack of an active partition.

Error codes: Numeric values displayed on the screen that alert the user to what is wrong with their system.

Error messages: Text strings displayed on the monitor that indicate what is wrong with the system.

Machine error: A machine error is associated with a hardware problem. Common problems include a defective hard drive, insufficient RAM, and a blown power supply.

Operator error: An operator error is associated with something that the user has done to produce a problem, such as deleting the files in the root directory by mistake.

System error: System errors are usually associated with the operating system or the system's environment. Common problems in this category include improper driver settings and corrupt system files.

Sample Questions

1. To determine whether a problem is due to a system or application error, you would do what?

A. Reinstall the application

B. Reinstall the operating system

C. Boot the system with a generic boot diskette

D. Boot the computer in Safe mode

Answer: C. Booting the system with a generic boot disk will bypass whatever entries are in the CONFIG.SYS and AUTOEXEC.BAT files as well as the OS on the hard drive.

2. Which of the following utilities can be used to fix most boot-up problems?

   A. FDISK /MBR

   B. FORMAT /MBR

   C. SYS

   D. SCANDISK

   Answer: A, C. FDISK /MBR will replace the master boot record with a general boot record, and SYS will restore the system files.

Recognize Windows-specific printing problems, and identify the procedures for correcting them.

This objective focuses on the problems that can occur with printers in a Windows environment. To be ready for this part of the exam, you will need to be familiar with the way Windows handles print jobs, know how to install and configure a printer for Windows, and be able to resolve common printer problems.

Critical Information

Installing and maintaining printers are two of the major task areas of a service technician. Installations are usually straightforward procedures with very few problems. With the installation utilities that come with most printers, the Printer Installation dialog box in Windows 3.*x*, and the Add Printer Wizard in Windows 95, installation is usually a no-brainer. However, problems do occasionally occur. Maintaining printers is also a relatively simple task, unless someone keeps tinkering with the settings.

In any case, you will need to be able to determine what is causing a particular printer problem and resolve it.

Basic Concepts of Windows Printing

From the OS view, printing under Windows consists of five basic components: the printer, the printer device driver, the computer's output port, the OS interface, and the hard disk drive.

The *printer* is, of course, the peripheral device you connect to the computer to provide hard-copy documents. Most modern printers have a built-in menu system that allows you to set the printer's configuration. These settings should coincide with the settings you initiate in the Windows environment.

The *device driver*, either the one that comes with the printer or the one provided by Windows, is the basic interface between the computer and the printer. It establishes the communications link with the OS and enables the OS to utilize the full range of features built into the printer. It is responsible for translating the print job into the data format the printer can use.

The *output port* (parallel or serial) is the physical connection point for the printer. It is also the logical connection point—the I/O port is assigned a memory address that the computer uses to transmit data to the printer and that the printer uses to signal the computer of its status.

The *OS interface* is the graphical device interface (GDI) that handles all the graphical input and output operations. The *disk drive* is used by Windows to store the temporary spool files.

Printing with Windows 3.*x* involves sending the print job to the GDI, which sends the job to the printer driver, which converts the data into a form the printer can use (Microsoft calls this the RAW data format).

After the translation, the print job is spooled to the disk drive, and the system is returned to the user. In the background, the print job is then spooled into the printer for printing.

In Windows 95, the print job is sent to the GDI, which creates an EMF (enhanced metafile format) file. The EMF files are smaller than the RAW files, faster to produce, and take up less space on the disk drive. Once the EMF file has been created, the system is returned to the user, and the file is spooled to the hard drive. The translation to RAW data is performed in the background as the file is spooled to the printer for printing.

NOTE   RAW data are simply raw data. The capitalization is Microsoft's way of contrasting them with the EMF data.

If you print documents generated by a 16-bit application under Windows 95, the virtual device drivers are used, which still give you the fast response time found with Windows 95 applications.

Troubleshooting Common Printer Problems

Printer problems are some of the most common problems facing a service technician in Windows 95. Many times, they will prove to be a major pain as well. You can use the Print Troubleshooter feature found in the help system of Windows 95 to assist you in resolving the more common printer problems (see Figure 4.2).

FIGURE 4.2: Windows 95 Print Troubleshooter

To activate the Print Troubleshooter:

1. Choose Start ➤ Help.

2. Click the Contents tab on the Help Topics screen.

3. Double-click the "If You Have Trouble Printing" option.

4. Answer the questions posed.

NOTE The Windows 95 CD-ROM version contains a more sophisticated Troubleshooter. It can be found in the \OTHER\MISC\EPTS folder. To execute it, double-click EPTS.EXE.

You should study all the entries in the Print Troubleshooter and have a well-grounded knowledge of the problems it was designed to fix. You should also read the C:\WINDOWS\PRINTERS.TXT file that comes with Windows 95.

The exam may cover the following areas:

Incorrect printer description in the Registry: Sometimes Windows 95 can read the PnP device wrong. In these cases, the printer's description in the Registry will be incorrect, and the printer will not work right. To fix this problem, delete the printer entry in the Device Manager and reboot your system. This will force Windows to reinstall the entry during the reboot process.

Hardware problems: Printing problems can be caused by not having the printer turned on or by having a defective printer cable. Check the hardware by trying to print directly to the printer with a DIR > LPT command at the DOS prompt. If it works, you can look at the print drivers.

Incorrect or incompatible device driver: Many times, the wrong printer driver has been installed, especially when you are trying emulation for an off-brand printer. Verify the settings with the technical documentation you received with your printer. To ensure you have a good copy of the driver, you can reinstall the printer.

Stalled print spool: A corrupted printer-driver file, using the wrong printer driver in your settings, or using the wrong settings for your spool configuration can cause stalled print spools. Check the settings for your printer to insure they are set properly, and check the spool settings. If the spooler is set to EMF format, change it to RAW (and vice versa) and try to print. You may also be trying to use EMF with a PostScript printer, which won't work. If your printer is a PostScript printer, you must set the spool option for RAW data.

Necessary Procedures

A service technician must also be familiar with printer installation. Setting up a printer in Windows 3.*x* and Windows 95 involves installing the print driver, then configuring the printer to system needs.

Installing a Windows 3.*x* Printer

You install a printer in Windows 3.*x* through the Control Panel.

1. Select the Printers icon.

2. Double-click the Add button to display the manufacturers and models for the Printers list.

3. Select the manufacturer and model of the printer from the Printers list, or select Install Unlisted or Updated Printer.

4. Configure your printer by selecting the Setup button to set the resolution and paper parameters, as shown below.

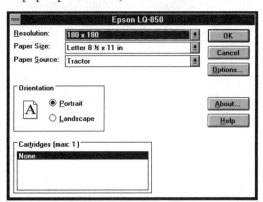

5. Set up your printer's connection by clicking the Connect button and selecting the port and timeouts, as shown below.

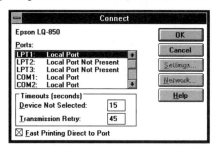

6. If it is a serial printer, you also need to define the settings for the COM port.

Installing a Windows 95 Printer

In Windows 95, you go to the Printers folder and double-click the Add Printer button. This will activate the Add Printer Wizard, which walks you through the installation procedure.

1. Designate whether the installation is for a local or network printer.

NOTE You should be connected and logged into the network before trying to install a network printer.

---

2. Select the printer's manufacturer and model from the Printers list, or click the Have Disk button.

3. Connect your printer to an available port.

4. As shown below, you will be asked to give a name for the installed printer. Naming it identifies it to the system, which will save the settings with the printer name.

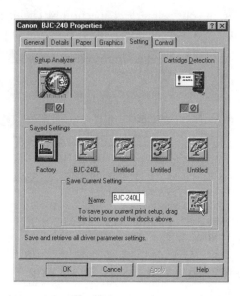

To configure a Windows 95 printer, go to the Printers folder, right-click the printer's icon, and select the Properties option. As shown below, this will display the Properties sheet for the printer. To find out the purpose for each entry on the sheet, right-click the property and then click the What's This? button that pops up.

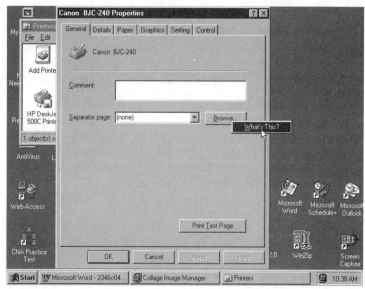

Exam Essentials

The "If You Have Trouble Printing" option is listed first on the Help Topics screen. This indicates that printing is one of the major sources of problems with Windows 95. You can definitely expect to see some questions regarding printer problems and what to do to fix them. The exam will certify your understanding and knowledge of the essential elements, operations, and troubleshooting techniques of the Windows printer subsystem.

Know how the printing process takes place in Windows 3.*x*.   In Windows 3.*x*, print jobs are sent to the GDI and then to the printer driver, which converts the file to RAW format and stores it in a spool file on the disk drive. The spool file is then sent to the printer for printing.

Know how the printing process takes place in Windows 95.   In Windows 95, print jobs are sent to the GDI, which creates an EMF file and sends it as a spool file to the disk drive. The printer driver then receives the EMF spool file and translates it to RAW format as the printer is printing the document.

Be familiar with the ways to install printer drivers in Windows. Windows 3.1 uses the Printers option in the Control Panel. Windows 95 uses the Add Printer Wizard in the Control Panel.

Key Terms and Concepts

EMF (enhanced metafile format):   A file format that is faster and easier to work with within the Windows 95 environment. It contains a higher-level 32-bit coding technology that is faster and more compact than other file formats.

Print job: A document that has been sent to the printer. Once the OS takes charge of it, the document is referred to as a print job.

RAW file: RAW data are actually raw data. Microsoft prefers to use capitalization to contrast them with EMF files. RAW is the data format that is actually sent to the printer for producing the hard copy of the document.

Spooling: Spooling a document involves off-loading the file from memory onto the disk drive, where it becomes a spool file. The spool file is a temporary holding area for files waiting to be printed. In Windows 3.*x*, spool files are RAW files; in Windows 95, they are EMF files.

Sample Questions

1. EMF is used in which of the following operating systems?

   A. DOS

   B. Windows 3.*x*

   C. Windows 95

   D. Windows 3.*x* and Windows 95

   Answer: C. The enhanced metafile format is used in Windows 95 printing operations.

2. What is the OS interface that handles printing in Windows?

   A. USER

   B. GDI

   C. IO.SYS

   D. VMM386

   Answer: B. GDI is the OS interface that receives the print job in both Windows 3.*x* and Windows 95.

Recognize common problems and determine how to resolve them.

T his objective concentrates on the most common errors that you will encounter when using Windows 95. It also covers the utilities you can use to troubleshoot, diagnose, and repair them.

Critical Information

Resolving computer problems is the basic purpose of the service technician's career. You have to enjoy problem solving and be able to think in a logical, orderly manner. Like any other skilled technician, you must be highly versed in the elements involved in your work (common problems) and the tools (utilities) used to perform your job tasks.

As a service technician, you will be faced with a wide variety of problems, some common and many not so common. If you know the causes of the most common problems, it will give insight into how to resolve them in a fast, effective manner. You will need to know the causes and solutions for the following problems:

- General protection faults (GPFs)
- Illegal operations
- Invalid working directory
- System lockup
- Nonfunctioning options
- Applications that refuse to start
- Inability to log onto a network

You will also need to be quite familiar with the tools of your trade. You must be able to use these tools for troubleshooting, diagnosing, and fixing the computer problems you will encounter. The tools provided by Microsoft include:

- SCANDISK.EXE
- ATTRIB.EXE
- EXTRACT.EXE
- DEFRAG.EXE
- EDIT.COM
- FDISK.EXE
- MSD.EXE
- MEM.EXE
- SYSEDIT.EXE
- Device Manager

The Most Common Problems and the Methods Used to Resolve Them

Computer systems are frustrating tools of productivity. Some work great for long periods of time, then without any warning they start to give all sorts of trouble. Others give you problems right out of the box. The only certain thing is that, sooner or later, they will give you a problem.

The source of any particular problem can be many different things. Some can be prevented, some cannot. Many times, you won't know what caused the problem or what you did to fix it.

This section covers the most common problems and defines the most probable causes for them. It will also provide you with some procedures that usually resolve the problem and bring the system back to operational status.

General Protection Faults

General protection faults (GPFs) are very common occurrences in Windows 3.*x* due to the basic design of the system and its inability to handle memory conflicts. GPFs are not nearly as common in Windows 95 due to its advanced 32-bit architecture and added control features.

A GPF error is associated with memory conflicts. A program that tries to use memory outside the memory addresses allocated to it is the basic cause of GPF errors. GPFs wreak havoc on the system by modifying the data stored in memory addresses used by other programs or the OS. As a result, applications and the OS can become unstable.

In Windows 3.x, the short-term solution is the use of Ctrl+Alt+Del to close the program, exit Windows, and reboot the system. A long-term diagnosis includes loading Dr. Watson and collecting some detailed information about what caused the GPF.

Troubleshooting methodology for Windows 3.x is as follows:

- Make sure that your hardware and network settings are correct and that there are no device conflicts, I/O port address conflicts, or conflicting TSR settings.

- Insure that you are using only Windows-compatible hardware devices and their Microsoft-approved drivers and TSRs. Contact the manufacturer for updated drivers and utilities.

- Determine whether you have a UMB or page mapping conflict. This can be done by starting Windows with the WIN /S or WIN /D:X commands. If this solves the problem, refer to the techniques described in Chapter 2 for resolving UMB conflicts.

- Ensure you are using the correct version of DOS. Windows requires that you use DOS 5 or later. In addition, some of the OEM versions are not totally compatible with machines made by other manufacturers and will cause memory problems. Upgrade to a current version of MS-DOS.

- Place the Dr. Watson diagnostic utility into the Startup group to collect information. Each time Dr. Watson detects an error, it writes pertinent information about the error to a file. It keeps a running record of all the active programs at the time of the fault and what you were trying to do when the error took place. Dr.

Watson can be modified in the WIN.INI file to tailor the information it collects. The information can be used to determine which programs or actions could be causing the GPFs.

Windows 95 does not experience many GPF errors. The situations that cause GPF errors in Windows 3.*x* now cause illegal-operation errors in Windows 95. In Windows 95, GPF errors are usually encountered when you have an upgrade version of Windows 95 that was installed on top of an existing Windows 3.*x* version. You will also discover that the cause of the GPF will be a DOS or Windows 3.*x* program or utility in one of the following situations:

- An application making a reference to a nonexistent memory address

- An application causing its attached API to return an error code

- An application trying to use memory allocated to another program

When Windows 95 comes across a GPF, it generates a message that alerts the user to the problem and includes the name of the application that caused the error, the module name, and a reference number. This information can be used to resolve the problem. You will need to contact the vendor or software publisher of the application and give them the information displayed with the error message. In most cases, they will send you an updated driver or module to install on your system.

The type of application that caused the problem will determine the actual effect a GPF has on your system.

- If the error was caused by a Windows 3.*x* (WIN16) program, all other WIN16 programs will stop working until the errant application is closed. Record the information provided by the error message and terminate the program. The application that had its memory space violated may also cause a problem if the errant program modified any of its data or program instructions.

- If a Windows 95 (WIN32) program caused the error, other programs should not be affected. Record the information and close the program.

- If a DOS program caused the error, there should be little effect on the operating system or other active applications. Record the information provided by the GPF error message and close the application.

Once you have the information that the error message gave you, contact the appropriate technical support personnel and let them help you. Many times, you will be given access to upgraded drivers.

The long-term solution is to replace all 16-bit (WIN16 and DOS) programs, utilities, and applications with Windows 95 versions, or contact the software publisher's technical support department, give them the details provided by the GPF error message, and follow their advice.

TIP Microsoft will provide you with a guide called *Troubleshooting GP Faults* if you call their FastTips hotline—(800) 936-4200. Place a request for a catalog; when you get it, order guide number WWW0524.

Illegal Operations

Programs (applications or utilities) that try to force their way into memory areas where they are not allowed cause *illegal-operation errors*. Usually, this error is produced when the program tries to step on some component of the OS.

In Windows 3.*x*, illegal-operation errors are caused when too many applications are open for the amount of memory available. The immediate solution is to close as many applications as possible, remove the wallpaper and backgrounds, and remove as many of the TSRs as you can. The long-range cure involves installing more memory.

In Windows 95, the problem is more complicated—16-bit and 32-bit applications, drivers, and utilities all run at the same time. The Virtual Machine Manager helps control this diverse group of programs, but sometimes a program manages to write data onto some other program's memory space. The short-term solution is to remove as many of the nonessential programs as possible. The long-range solution requires you to add more memory or acquire upgraded drivers, especially for the 16-bit programs.

Your DLL (dynamic link library) files can also produce the illegal-operation error message. These files are commonly used procedures, which supply support to many different applications. Most applications have their own set of DLLs that are specifically designed for the application.

When you add a new program to your system, their DLLs will often be copied into the Windows directory and may overwrite existing system DLLs. These new DLLs may not be compatible with the other applications that the old versions supported. If you have just installed a new program and your other programs start to give you illegal-operation errors, you can be pretty certain that the new application has replaced some of the more compatible DLLs in your system. Usually the only way to correct this problem is to reinstall the OS. The long-range plan is one of prevention. To prevent installation overwrites of your DLLs:

- Use an installation shell utility such as WINDELETE by IMSI— (800) 833-0935. This type of software will filter the new application's installation process and track all the changes it makes to your system. If you need to delete the new application, the utility facilitates the process by removing all the program fragments from wherever they are in your system. It will also replace the new DLL files with the original ones.

- If the installation utility gives you an option for a preferred directory for shared files, indicate that you want them in the new application's directory.

- Back up your entire C:\WINDOWS\SYSTEM directory prior to installing the new application. If things go wrong, restore the backup to your system. In Windows 95, it is a good idea to back up the USER.DAT and SYSTEM.DAT files as well.

> **NOTE** Duplicate or incompatible DLL files can also cause *fatal-exception errors*. When you get one of these, do not save your work under the same filename—you will probably trash the file.

Invalid Working Directory

Invalid-working-directory errors are usually associated with a broken network connection. When you log onto an active network and start working in a network drive, you are using an extension of the network's resources. If the connection is broken, your workstation computer can no longer access the drive. When you try to access the drive, you will get an invalid-working-directory error message. Some of the more common reasons for this problem are as follows:

- In any network environment, a defective cable or interface card could cause a problem. To solve these problems, check to see whether other systems have been affected, then check the server and the cabling. Restart the server if needed and replace any defective cards or cables.

- In a peer-to-peer network, if someone turns off the computer that has the drive you are referencing for use, it could cause the problem. If this is the problem, simply restart the computer and reconnect to the drive.

- In a client/server network, a crashed server could cause the problem. If this is the case, all the other computers connected to the server will also be affected. Connection is possible only after the server has been restored.

System Lockups

Improper management of the UMB region, corrupted files, defective or obsolete device drivers, or defective hardware usually cause *system lockups*. Some of the things you can do to resolve these problems are as follows:

- Ensure that all your hardware is working properly. If possible, swap out devices with other devices from a working system.

- Work with the UMB region. In DOS/Windows 3.*x*, you may be able to fix the problem by using MEMMAKER. However, Windows 95 does not have that option. Try rearranging the order of the command lines that load your 16-bit drivers and TSRs.

TIP   Use a generic boot disk to help you determine whether you have a UMB conflict. REM out all the entries in the AUTOEXEC.BAT and CONFIG.SYS files. Then, add them back one at a time, rebooting each time one is added. If the system locks up after you have added a command line, the driver or TSR that you just loaded is the cause of your problem.

- If you have tested the drivers and TSRs and the system still locks up, obtain and install the latest drivers and patches for all of the hardware and software you have installed in your system.

Application Keeps Crashing

This problem is caused by a missing or corrupted DLL or INI file, an incompatible device driver, or defective hardware. To fix this type of problem:

- Ensure that the hardware is operational by swapping it out with equipment that you know is good

- Reinstall the hardware driver with the latest version from the manufacturer

- Reinstall the application

- Reinstall Windows

Option Will Not Function

Bugs in the software or corrupted files are the most common causes for failure of an option or its erratic behavior. This problem can also be caused by improper settings in the PIF used to activate the application. These problems can be fixed by:

- Installing the latest software patches from the software publisher

- Reinstalling the application that is giving you trouble

- Modifying the PIF settings, especially those dealing with the display

---

NOTE   If you are in a DOS program that is running under Windows 3.*x*, the mouse option will not work unless you have the mouse driver loaded into memory through either the CONFIG.SYS or the AUTOEXEC.BAT files.

Application Will Not Start or Load

When a DOS-based application fails to run or load into memory, you can expect a problem with your video driver. You may be using the wrong driver, it may be corrupted, or it may have a bug in it. When a Windows-based application fails to run, a corrupted application file is probably the cause. To repair this type of problem:

- Reinstall the drivers and/or get the latest patches and install them.

- Use the standard VGA driver provided by Windows.

Windows Does Not Run Properly

When Windows 3.*x* starts acting strangely, the suspects include a corrupted file or an unstable system. An unstable system can be caused by an unreported GPF or by using one or more damaging DOS commands. To solve this problem:

- Perform a cold boot (power off) of your system, which will restore the system from a GPF, and see what happens. If it still acts weird, you may need to reinstall Windows.

- Do not use the APPEND, FASTOPEN, GRAPHICS, JOIN, or MODE (to change video modes) commands. These commands will interfere with the way Windows wants to do things. In addition, some commands such as MIRROR can cause problems with disk activities. Virus checkers have also been known to cause some problems. You will have to work with these commands and utilities to determine how your system will accept them.

Windows Displays an Application-Execution Error When Trying to Run the Application from the File Manager or Program Manager
This problem is caused by the lack of a listing for the application's directory path in the system variables. This problem is solved by:

- Inserting the application's directory into the PATH= statement in AUTOEXEC.BAT.

- Inserting the application's directory location in the Working Directory field of the application's Properties sheet.

Unrecoverable-Application Error (UAE)
These errors are caused by a lack of sufficient memory to run the application or a lack of sufficient environment space. This type of problem is resolved by:

- Modifying the application's PIF so that it has enough memory to run.

- Creating a PIF for the application that will increase the environment space. This is done by entering COMMAND.COM in the Program Name field and putting the following line in the Optional Parameters field: /E 1024 /C *directory path/filename*, where *directory path* is the drive and directory to the application, and *filename* is the name of the application.

Cannot Log onto Network
Inability to log onto a network is usually caused by defective or missing network drivers or utilities, defective cabling or network interface card, not having a login account, or using the wrong password. To resolve these problems:

- Reinstall the drivers.

- Ensure that the cabling and network interface card (NIC) are functional.

- Make sure you have a network account for the server, and that you are using the correct login name and password.

Utilities for Troubleshooting, Diagnosing, and Resolving Problems

Microsoft includes a large inventory of utilities that can be used to troubleshoot, diagnose, and repair problems with your computer. Knowing how to use them is essential to your success and productivity as a service technician.

ATTRIB.EXE

ATTRIB is used to set the attributes of a file. The attributes are Read Only, Archive, System, and Hidden. The attributes tell the system how to handle the file (e.g., if a file is Read Only, the system will prevent you from changing the contents of the file or deleting the file). Figure 4.3 shows the options available for ATTRIB.

FIGURE 4.3: ATTRIB options

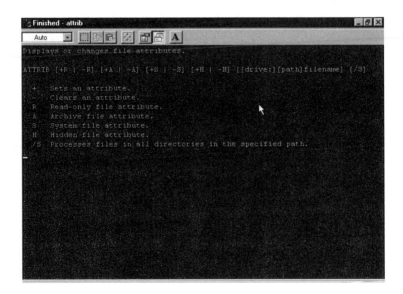

Read Only: This option sets (+R) or clears (–R) the Read Only attribute bit. When set, the Read Only attribute allows the file to be read, but protects it from modification and deletion.

CONFIG.SYS and AUTOEXEC.BAT are excellent candidates for this attribute.

Archive: This option will set (+A) or clear (–R) the Archive bit. This attribute is essential for most backup systems. Modifying a file will set the Archive bit, and backing up the file will clear it.

System: This option will set (+A) or clear (–R) the System bit. The OS uses this bit to mark the file for special handling.

Hidden: This option will set (+A) or clear (–R) the Hidden bit. The Hidden bit prevents the file from being read in a regular DIR directory listing.

The specific process for launching ATTRIB differs with the operating system you are using. With DOS, you simply enter the ATTRIB command string at the system prompt. For Windows 3.x and Windows 95, you have to use the file's Properties sheet to set the attributes.

DEFRAG.EXE

DEFRAG is used to rearrange disk files into contiguous blocks on the disk drive. On a new disk drive, the OS stores files in contiguous clusters. During normal use, the drive fills up, and you delete files that you no longer need. As new files are added to the drive, the OS will fill up the holes in storage left by the files you deleted, which will break longer files into smaller segments. Having files segmented in this manner is called *fragmentation*. As fragmentation increases, your disk drive's performance decreases due to the excessive amount of access time needed to gather the information from all the fragments of the file.

DEFRAG restores the drive's performance by rearranging each of the files into its own single, contiguous block, which eliminates all the added access time needed to look for the many scattered pieces of a file.

For both DOS and Windows 3.x, DEFRAG must be run from the DOS prompt. Windows 95 allows you to launch it from the regular OS without having to reboot into the DOS Only mode. Figure 4.4 shows the Windows 95 DEFRAG screen.

F I G U R E 4.4: Windows 95 DEFRAG screen

EDIT.COM

EDIT is a text editor used extensively in creating and modifying the CONFIG.SYS and AUTOEXEC.BAT files. EDIT is part of QBASIC, which must be present before EDIT will work.

In Windows 3.*x* and Windows 95, the editor of choice is NOTEPAD, but EDIT can still be used. Windows 95 has modified NOTEPAD so that it is a stand-alone program and no longer requires QBASIC. See Figure 4.5 for a picture of the EDIT utility screen.

F I G U R E 4.5: EDIT screen

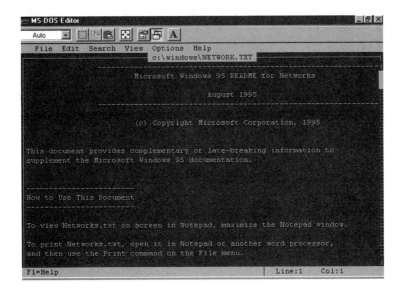

EXTRACT.EXE

EXTRACT is used to expand compressed installation files in Windows 95 onto your system. If you have corrupt or missing files, you will use the EXTRACT utility/command to replace the files from the installation disk set.

In DOS and Windows 3.*x*, you would use the EXPAND command to expand the compressed files and put them onto your hard drive. Figure 4.6 shows the syntax and options available with the EXTRACT command.

FIGURE 4.6: The EXTRACT command

FDISK.EXE

As shown in Figure 4.7, FDISK is used to partition hard disk drives. OEM drives must be partitioned before you can format them. FDISK /MBR is used to repair the master boot record (MBR) if it becomes corrupted or is destroyed by a virus. Using FDISK will irretrievably destroy any data on the drive.

F I G U R E 4.7: FDISK main menu options

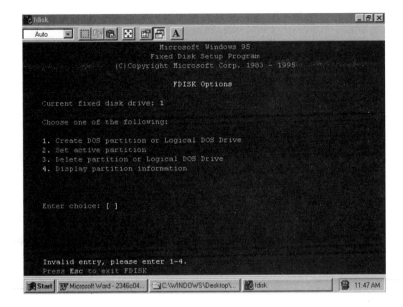

MEM.EXE

MEM is used to examine the way the system is utilizing RAM memory. As you can see in Figure 4.8, MEM displays how much of each type of memory is available and how much is used. If you use MEM /C, it will display which programs are loaded into the different memory areas.

MSD.EXE

MSD is Microsoft Diagnostics and is used to display system information. It is available with DOS version 6.*x* and Windows 3.1, but is not available in Windows 95—MSD must be used in the DOS environment. If used from within Windows, it will produce unreliable results. The entry screen for MSD is shown in Figure 4.9.

FIGURE 4.8: The MEM output display

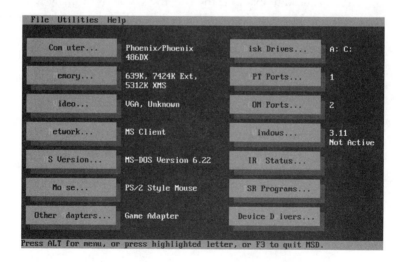

FIGURE 4.9: MSD entry screen

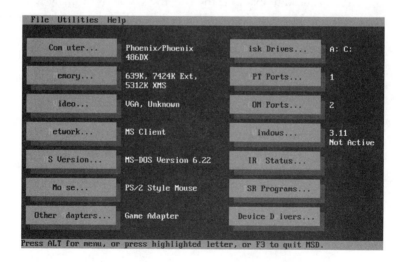

REGEDIT.EXE

REGEDIT is used in Windows to make adjustments to the Registry. A powerful Find feature allows you to search for instances of a particular driver that you can change or delete. Do not make any changes in the Registry unless you know exactly what you are doing and have made a backup of the USER.DAT and SYSTEM.DAT files. The Windows 95 REGEDIT screen is shown in Figure 4.10.

F I G U R E 4.10: REGEDIT utility

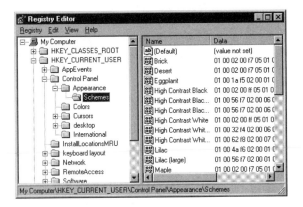

SCANDISK.EXE

SCANDISK is used to repair broken partitions, FAT, and unallocated clusters. As Figure 4.11 indicates, SCANDISK also has an optional feature for checking and analyzing the surface of the disk drive for defective spots. In the process, it recovers any data in the defective areas if it can.

In DOS and Windows 3.*x*, you must run the SCANDISK utility from the DOS prompt. In Windows 95, it can run within the GUI operating system.

SYSEDIT.EXE

SYSEDIT is a Windows-based text editor. As shown in Figure 4.12, it displays all of the text-based system files for editing. CONFIG.SYS, AUTOEXEC.BAT, WIN.INI, and SYSTEM.INI are by default the files displayed. If you have a network or other features installed on your system, other files may be displayed as well, such as PROTOCOL.INI.

FIGURE 4.11: Windows 95 SCANDISK options screen

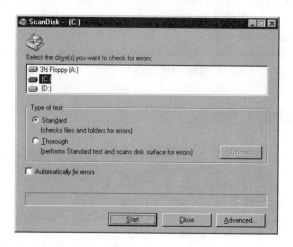

FIGURE 4.12: SYSEDIT window

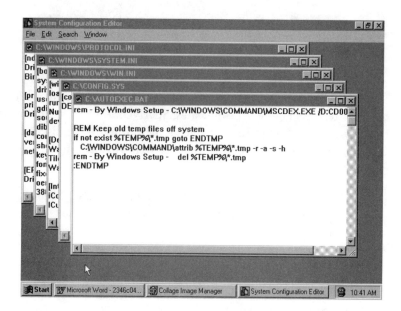

GUI-Based Features for Troubleshooting, Diagnosing, and Resolving Problems

In addition to the utilities listed above, Windows 95 has a couple of GUI-based features that help you troubleshoot your system. These features are the Device Manager and the Performance tab on the System Properties folder in the Control Panel.

Device Manager

The Device Manager in Windows 95 is a tab found on the System Properties page in the Control Panel. It is used to locate and resolve hardware conflicts in Windows 95 (see Figure 4.13).

FIGURE 4.13: The Device Manager

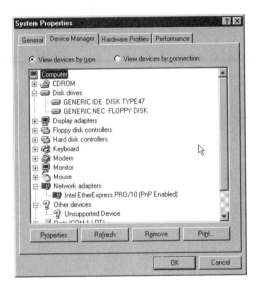

The first level of the display is the device class. These icons represent the basic types of devices installed on your computer. The second level of icons represents each of the installed devices for the specific device type.

If a device is in conflict with another device, it will be marked with an exclamation mark (!) within a yellow circle. If a device is not working properly, it will be marked with a forward slash (/) within a red circle.

A device that Windows has located but could not identify is marked with a yellow question mark (?) and the label Other Devices.

Performance Tab

The Performance tab (see Figure 4.14) is also located on the System Properties sheet. It helps you keep track of how much of the system's resources are still available, and lets you know whether you are running any 16-bit device drivers.

FIGURE 4.14: The Performance tab

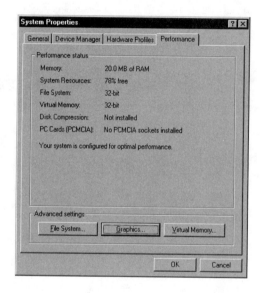

The Performance tab allows you to optimize your graphics display, hard disk drive, CD-ROM, and virtual memory settings. It can also be used to help troubleshoot display and drive problems.

Exam Essentials

The A+ exam will test your knowledge of troubleshooting principles and concepts. It will also focus on the more common problems, their causes, and the more readily available solutions.

Be familiar with the causes and solutions of the most common problems. The most common problems facing a service technician are GPFs, illegal operations, invalid working directories, system lockups, options that refuse to function, applications that refuse to start or load, and the inability to log onto the network.

Be familiar with the major tools that you will need to use in troubleshooting, diagnosing, and resolving problems. The tools you will use to troubleshoot, diagnose, and fix problems include SCANDISK, ATTRIB, EXTRACT, DEFRAG, EDIT, FDISK, MSD, MEM, and SYSEDIT. These tools are utilities supplied by Microsoft with the OS. In Windows 95, you will extensively use the Device Manager for resolving your system problems.

Key Terms and Concepts

API (Application Program Interface): A program that contains a set of programming protocols that dictates an application's behavior.

Client/server network: A network with a dedicated file server that provides services to the workstations (clients) that request the services. See also *Network*.

Crashed server: A server that has unexpectedly gone down without being scheduled.

Network: Two or more computers connected together in such a way as to share files and system resources.

OEM drives: Hard drives that are not partitioned or formatted.

OEM version: The software supplied by the vendor. Normally this term is used to describe an OS that has been modified for a particular computer manufacturer. OEM versions are modified to work on specific computer types and may not work well on computers by another manufacturer.

Patch: A segment of a program that has been created to fix a bug in the software. The software publisher usually provides these free of charge.

Peer-to-peer network: A network with no dedicated server. All of the workstations on the network provide and receive services from each other. See also *Network*.

Sample Questions

1. You have a DOS program running within Windows 3.*x* that has just attempted to access memory allocated to another program. Which error code would you expect to be displayed?

   A. General protection fault

   B. Illegal-operation error

   C. Fatal-exception error

   D. Memory-allocation error

   Answer: A. In Windows 3.*x*, the GPF is used to indicate that a program is trying to use another program's memory addresses.

2. Which utility would be used to restore the master boot record on the hard drive?

   A. SCANDISK

   B. DEFRAG

   C. FDISK

   D. FIXDISK

   Answer: C. FDISK /MBR is used to replace the master boot record.

Identify concepts relating to viruses and virus types—their danger, their symptoms, sources of viruses, how they infect, how to protect against them, and how to identify and remove them.

This objective focuses on your knowledge of viruses—what you can do to remove them from your system and how to safeguard your system from infection.

Critical Information

Viruses and other rogue-type software are a significant threat in today's computing environment. Your system is vulnerable to attacks by viruses, Trojan horses, worms, and logic bombs. Unless your computer is completely isolated from things like the Internet, bulletin boards, and floppy diskettes, you will experience an unwanted intrusion sooner or later. Like jury duty, it's only a matter of time before you get selected.

If you know how viruses work, the symptoms they produce, and the potential damages they can do, it will help you effectively deal with the threat.

Overview of Viruses

Miscreant software is the classification for programs that are designed to do mischief within a computer system. They are intruders that gain entrance to the system illegally. They pose a threat to the system and the data and applications stored in it, or take up resources that could be used for other needs.

The following things can threaten your system:

Logic bombs: Logic bombs are small programs—once they gain entrance to your system, they wait until one or more of your system's variables reach a trigger value. At that time, they will release their payload, which is usually designed for massive destruction.

Software bombs: Software bombs are also small programs—once they get into your system, they immediately activate their destructive payload.

Trojan horses: Trojan horses are the granddaddies of all rogue software. They are programs that are designed to look like some other program to spur the curiosity of a user into using them. Once inside, they will deliver a payload from a mild message to massive destruction of files.

Worms: Worms are secret little programs normally associated with networks or large, multiuser systems. They crawl around your system gathering information and leaving back doors to the system. These back doors can later be used to gain unauthorized access to the system without going through the normal system procedures.

Viruses: Viruses are small programs designed to replicate themselves into other programs. They are the only rogue-type software that clone themselves. In most cases, their payload is destructive.

For the vast majority of users, the term *virus* has grown to encompass all of the different types of miscreant software. Generally speaking, viruses have grown in popularity, while the other types of miscreant software have lost their popularity. The rest of this section will deal specifically with the true viruses (i.e., the ones whose primary goal is to clone themselves).

Most modern viruses can hide themselves from antivirus software. The three ways that a virus can cloak itself are as follows:

Encryption: An encrypting virus hides itself by changing into non-cloning program code. Since virus seekers look for code that performs replications, in its dormant, nonreproductive state, the virus is invisible to the antivirus software.

Polymorphism: Polymorphic viruses modify their signatures each time they reproduce. This mutative ability keeps them one jump ahead of the virus seekers who look for the distinguishing features of the virus. This ability is the reason you need to constantly upgrade your antivirus program.

Stealth: Stealth viruses camouflage themselves by modifying the infected file's characteristics to report back to the OS the same date, time, file size, and checksum. Since most antivirus programs keep track of this information, the virus can go undetected. Another way that the stealth virus operates is to monitor the OS's calls for files. If the file it is in is called, the virus removes itself from the file or has the OS load an uninfected copy of the file that it keeps on hand for this purpose.

There are four stages in the progression of a viral infection:

Local memory infection: The virus enters the computer through an infected program file and takes up residence in memory. At this stage, the virus is benign and will infect very few files. This stage is also known as the incubation period. At this stage, you can get rid of the virus by performing a cold boot with a clean boot diskette and running the antivirus removal program. You may also have to repair the damage to the file's structure by running CHKDSK or SCANDISK. You should also isolate the offending virus diskette, or download and destroy it.

Local disk storage infection: At this stage, the virus goes into its aggressive phase and infects everything it can. Some will infect only a predetermined number of files before dumping their payloads and destroying themselves. During this stage, there will be loss of data, scrambled FAT, damaged partitions, and corrupted files. If the virus is caught soon enough, the system can be restored by eliminating the virus with an antivirus program, reinstalling affected applications, reinstalling the OS, and using a data-recovery tool. If the virus is left alone for too long, the system will be totally destroyed and will require repartitioning, reformatting, and reinstallation of the OS and applications. Do not rely on backups to restore the system—they may also be infected.

Shared file system infection: If you are on a network and have a system of shared files, they can become infected by workstations that are infected. This is the exponential growth stage of the virus. In a very short period of time, the virus can infect hundreds or even thousands of machines. At this point, severe measures are called for to stop the spread. The server and all workstations must be powered down, and each one carefully and completely checked for and cleared of any viruses. All removable media must be checked for viruses as well. This recovery will be time consuming, tedious, and costly.

Systemwide infection of removable media: At this stage, complete recovery is almost impossible. Draconian measures must be taken to limit damage. All existing removable media, such as floppies and tapes, need to be destroyed. The use of personal diskettes, tapes, and CDs needs to be curtailed. All systems need to have current virus checkers on them at all times, and workstations need to have antivirus programs run at frequent intervals.

There are three basic types of viruses based on the areas that they infect: the boot-sector virus, the file-infector virus, and the multipartite virus.

Boot-Sector Viruses

Boot-sector viruses write themselves into the master boot record of a hard drive or floppy diskette. During boot up, they load themselves into memory and copy themselves to the boot sector of the diskette in the floppy drive whenever a read or write call is made to the floppy.

Getting rid of boot-sector viruses can be a trying experience. You can repartition the hard drive and reformat a floppy, but some of the viruses in this category will not be removed without the help of an antivirus program.

The best system defense for this type of virus is prevention. You need to:

- Never leave a diskette in the floppy drive. This will prevent the system from trying to boot from the floppy drive.

  - If you do have a nonbootable diskette in the drive and the system tries to boot from it, do not remove the diskette and then let the system continue to boot. Instead, remove the diskette, turn off the computer, and turn it back on again. This will insure that the virus will not be in memory. A Ctrl+Alt+Del (warm boot) will not initialize all of the memory segments.

- Set your CMOS to boot from the hard drive first and the A: drive second. This will take care of the times you leave a diskette in the floppy drive. This option is not available on all versions of CMOS.

- Set your CMOS settings to prevent any writes to the boot sector of the hard drive. This will prevent all but the most clever boot-sector viruses from infecting the hard drive. Any attempts to write will be thwarted and will display a warning message on the screen.

File-Infector Viruses

File-infector viruses are viruses that infect executable files (namely the EXE and COM files). They also can infect the macros of a word-processor application. The data file itself is not infected and cannot be used to replicate the virus. A document macro is a small program within the document that can be executed when the document is first loaded or later by pressing the key that activates the macro.

File infectors wait in memory for other suitable programs to come along. When they perform a disk write operation, the file infector will replicate itself within the program's disk file or will create another file with the same name, but with a COM extension. This COM file is then used by the OS to launch the program, but it loads the virus into memory instead. The virus then calls the real program and waits in memory for the opportunity to clone itself into another program.

Some of the viruses in this category target specific system files such as COMMAND.COM, IO.SYS, and MSDOS.SYS. Others are designed to target specific applications such as Microsoft products.

Current antivirus programs are the only way to get rid of these viruses. The antivirus program will read the code of all executable program files, checking for the virus signatures it has on file.

The only way to prevent getting infected by a file-infector virus is to isolate your machine from Internet downloads, floppy disks, and CD-ROMs. Short of this, you need to scan every program and file that you put into your computer before you install them.

Multipartite Viruses

Multipartite viruses infect both the boot sector and the executable files you have on the system. Most of these viruses target system files and the master boot sector.

These viruses can be caught by booting from an A: drive that has an infected diskette, downloading an infected file from the Internet, or activating an infected program from a floppy.

Antivirus programs can be used to exterminate multipartite viruses from your system. To prevent being infected by these viruses, you should follow the steps listed in both the boot-sector and file-infector sections above.

How Viruses Are Spread

Viruses are highly contagious. In a matter of hours, they can infect thousands of machines. The major avenues of infection are through your computer's modem, the floppy drive, and the CD-ROM drive. Everything that comes across these media should be suspect and needs to be thoroughly tested before use. This includes packaged software from reputable dealers. The user activities that increase the risk of exposure to viral attacks include:

- Connecting your computer to a network that doesn't have a network version of an antivirus program

- Using shared application files from a network—especially an unprotected one

- Swapping programs on floppy disks with friends or relatives

- Purchasing software from lesser-known, unproven vendors

- Downloading applications, utilities, and word-processor documents that contain macros from the Internet or a BBS (bulletin board system)

- Using reformatted diskettes that haven't been checked for viruses

- Using pirated software

Symptoms of Viruses

The symptoms produced by a virus infection are often obscure and difficult to pin down. Without an antivirus program, determining whether you have a viral infection is nearly impossible. Most of the symptoms are the same for a piece of hardware getting ready to check out, a corrupted application, or a faulty OS. Many virus attacks go unreported due to the user believing there is something wrong with the computer itself or that they have done something wrong. Some of the more common symptoms that should lead you to believe you have a viral infection include:

- Your antivirus program reports that you have a possible virus

- A program takes longer to load than normal, or you notice an excessive amount of hard drive activity

- Available system resources are suddenly reduced

- The OS cannot access the hard or CD-ROM drive

- Executable program files undergo unexplained increases in size

- You have frequently recurring problems with corrupted or missing files or device drivers

- The amount of bad sectors on the hard drive suddenly increases

- The system hangs right after it starts reading the hard drive while booting the system

- FAT and partition-table error messages are displayed
- Strange graphics or messages appear on the screen
- Your OS becomes unstable and unreliable

Preventive Measures

Antivirus programs alone cannot stop virus infections. The user (and the way they handle their system) is the first line of defense against virus attacks. To help them in their efforts at prevention, you can do the following things:

- Install an up-to-date antivirus program on each machine and the network—nothing beats a good antivirus program. To be effective, though, it must be kept current.

NOTE   Antivirus software should be able to automatically load during the boot process, automatically monitor downloads, automatically scan word-processing documents for macro viruses, and download virus updates on a regular basis.

- Give your users some solid training in antivirus techniques. Show them what to do and what not to do to prevent, stop, and report virus attacks.

- Keep the system physically secure. Do not let anyone and everyone have access to a computer. Keep unauthorized personnel away. There have been cases where employees have let their children do homework on their office machine, and the diskette used had a virus that infected over half the computers in the department before anyone realized what was happening.

- Create company-wide policies that govern the safe use of computers, including the prevention and reporting of virus attacks. Make sure the policy has high-level management backing and some form of punch so that users take notice.

Necessary Procedures

When you have a virus, you must act swiftly and decisively before the virus has a chance to spread outside controllable bounds. Failure to act quickly could prove fatal for the company. With that in mind, here are the procedures that you should follow to eliminate a virus from your system.

Removing a Virus from a Single Computer

Hopefully, this is the only type of virus-related problem that you will encounter (on a single machine), but it could be merely a step in the overall process of eliminating a virus from your corporation. In the latter case, you will have to perform this operation on every machine in your company before you can get rid of a virus. Whatever the case may be, follow the procedure below.

1. Keep calm. Don't panic. Use your head.

2. Stop processing immediately and turn off the computer.

3. Identify the extent of the infection. Did it come from a single disk or did it come from the shared files on the network? If it came from the latter, jump to the next procedure: "Removing a Virus from a Network."

4. Reboot the system with a clean boot diskette.

5. Run a virus-removal program.

6. Back up all data files.

7. Repartition the hard drive (proceed with this step only if needed).

8. Reformat the hard drive.

9. Reinstall the OS from clean copies of the originals.

10. Reinstall all software from clean copies of the originals.

11. Restore the data back onto the system.

12. Reconfigure the system to your needs.

Removing a Virus from a Network

As mentioned earlier, the viral infestation may have spread throughout the entire company. If it has, you must suspect the network is infected as well. Here's the best method to proceed with when you expect the network is infected:

1. Keep calm. Don't panic. Use your head.

2. Activate your emergency recovery team. What? No team! Do the best you can, but don't expect miracles.

3. Suspend processing on all workstations, servers, and stand-alone systems. Turn them off and follow the procedures described for removing a virus from a single machine on each and every computer in the corporation. Keep a detailed log of the machines you have to check, and sign off on the log after completing the check and removing any viruses on a machine. It is also a good idea to tag the computer as "Cleaned" with a date and the signature of the person who did the check.

4. Determine whether the infection has spread outside the company. If it has, alert all possible victims of the increased risk. When you inform them, try to be as specific as possible as to what files were infected.

5. Collect and isolate all removable media, test them, and clean them or toss them.

6. Do not continue processing until the server and all workstations have been tested, cleaned, and declared ready to go by the emergency recovery team.

Exam Essentials

The A+ exam will test your knowledge of common virus problems and the methods used to detect and clean them.

Know the primary symptoms of a virus. Virus infections usually produce the following symptoms: abnormal time periods or disk access times, unusual messages, corrupted or missing files, an unstable system, sudden reduction in system resources, and the inability to access a hard or CD-ROM drive.

Be familiar with the major methods by which a computer becomes infected. Basically, be doubly suspicious of everything except software that you have just tested. The most common ways of infection include downloads from the Internet or a BBS and using untested floppy diskettes.

Key Terms and Concepts

Boot-sector virus: A virus that infects the boot record on a disk drive or floppy diskette.

Encrypting virus: A virus that hides itself by encrypting its signature.

File-infector virus: A virus that will stay in memory after it infects executable files such as COM and EXE files.

Logic bomb: A miscreant program that activates only when one or more of the system variables meet a predetermined value.

Macro virus: A type of virus that infects the macros of a word-processing or spreadsheet document.

Memory-resident virus: A virus that stays in memory after its host program terminates.

Multipartite virus: A virus that shares the characteristics of boot-sector and file-infector viruses.

Nonmemory-resident virus: A virus that terminates with its host program.

Payload: The purpose for which the virus was designed. Some payloads are simple "You Been Had" messages, while others perform massive destruction to disk files.

Polymorphic virus: A virus that mutates itself during the replication phase.

Replicator: A virus whose payload is to reproduce itself so rapidly that it bogs down the system. Also known as a rabbit virus.

Signature: The identifiable characteristics of a virus. The signature is usually the code that allows the virus to reproduce itself.

Software bomb: Miscreant program that will start devastation as soon as it is loaded into memory.

Stealth virus: A virus that hides itself by insuring that the file attributes for the host have not been changed, or by presenting an uninfected copy of the host when called by the OS.

Time bomb: Miscreant program that has a specific time structure to follow before it activates, such as Friday the 13th. It is a type of logic bomb.

Trojan horse: Miscreant program that poses as something it isn't. When loaded, it keeps people busy trying to work with it while it destroys files in the background, loads worms, or sets up back doors into the system.

Virus: Miscreant program whose single distinguishing feature is the ability to clone itself into the code of another program.

Worm: Miscreant program designed to roam through a system collecting information and setting up false accounts. Most do no outright damage themselves, but allow their creator easy access into the system.

Sample Questions

1. What do you call a virus that infects both the boot record and an executable file?

   A. Polymorphic virus

   B. Multipartite virus

   C. Stealth virus

   D. Trojan horse

   Answer: B. A virus that infects both the boot record and an executable file is called a multipartite virus.

2. What is the signature of a virus?

   A. The result of what happens when the virus activates

   B. The specific characteristics of the virus

   C. The code changes within the host program that allow the virus to reside there

   D. None of the above

   Answer: B. The signature of a virus is its identifiable characteristics. This is what a virus-hunter program looks for when it searches files for a virus.

CHAPTER

5

Networks

A+ Exam Objectives Covered in This Chapter:

▶ **Identify the networking capabilities of DOS and Windows, including procedures for connecting to the network.**
(pages 222 – 232)

▶ **Identify concepts and capabilities relating to the Internet and basic procedures for setting up a system for Internet access.**
(pages 233 – 241)

This domain covers the concepts, capabilities, and procedures associated with local area networks (LANs) and the Internet. The major purpose of this domain of the examination is to test your knowledge of network operating systems (NOSs) and the protocols used to connect to the Internet.

Although a lot of material can be covered in each of the objectives in this domain, the A+ exam will touch only lightly on these areas. Know what a network is, how it is put together, and the protocols that are used for communications. You should also know how to set up drives, files, and printers for network sharing.

NOTE This material comprises 10 percent of the exam. It also represents skills that are very much in demand.

▶ Identify the networking capabilities of DOS and Windows, including procedures for connecting to the network.

This objective concentrates on local area networks (LANs) and their capabilities. In particular, it focuses on peer-to-peer networks and the capabilities that DOS and Windows have for networking.

Critical Information

Networking is a rapidly growing area in the computer industry. Just about every business has some sort of network installed. Many smaller firms are using peer-to-peer LANs. By learning the concepts and procedures covered in this section, you will be able to install, configure, and maintain these networks.

Classifications of Networks

There are several ways to classify networks. The most common are by type of deployment, type of topology, type of standard, and type of protocol. Networks can be classified by deployment in two basic categories: *client/server* and *peer to peer*.

Client/server networks: Two or more computers connected together for the purpose of communications, increased productivity, and the sharing of resources. Client/server networks have a dedicated file server that provides services to the client workstations connected to the network. Client/server networks should be installed when you need to network more than 10 workstations. This deployment method is more expensive due to the additional cost of a dedicated server, but the efficiency of the network can be maintained.

Peer-to-peer networks: Two or more computers connected together for the purpose of sharing system resources and communications. Each computer shares designated resources with each other computer. All computers act as servers and clients. As servers, they provide services; as clients, they request services. Peer-to-peer networks should usually be used when there are from five to 10 computers that need to be networked. As the number of computers increases on this type of network, the efficiency of the network decreases.

Many smaller companies are using Windows 3.11 (Windows for Workgroups) and Windows 95 to set up peer-to-peer LANs within their businesses. Since small businesses account for over 80 percent of the total number of businesses in the United States, you probably will be working on one of these smaller networks. Some of the advantages associated with peer-to-peer LANs include:

- They are cost effective—the capability of networking is already built into Windows 3.11 and Windows 95. Only a relatively small cash outlay is needed to purchase the network cards and cabling.

- They are fairly easy to install and set up.

- There is no requirement for a certified network technician to administer and maintain the system.

- Large outlays of money for training are not needed. The network is part of the OS, and the common user interface facilitates learning the new network features and the procedures for getting them to run.

- They give you the ability to connect people in workgroups and set them up into project teams with each team having their own set of shared files and resources.

On the downside, the disadvantages include:

- An overall drop in system performance due to each computer sharing designated resources with other workgroup members

- A lack of proper security for sensitive or proprietary information

- The disruption of workgroup operations when a member fails to show up for work and their computer is unavailable

Networks are also classified by their physical layout or *topology*. All networks are connected together using one of the following topologies: *star, bus, ring,* or *hybrid*.

Star topology: A star topology connects its workstations together from a single, central point. The central point can be either a file server (called the host) or an active hub. The file server would be used in a client/server setup; the active hub would be used for a peer-to-peer LAN. Star topologies are most often associated with ArcNet networks.

Bus topology: This topology connects workstations together with a single length of cable that is terminated on both ends. Bus topologies are used with both client/server and peer-to-peer networks. Bus topologies are most intimately identified with Ethernet networks.

Ring topology: A ring topology connects its workstations together as a single, end-connected-to-end ring. Ring topologies are most closely associated with IBM Token Ring networks.

Hybrid topology: A hybrid is a combination of any of the three other types of topologies. Hybrid topologies are found in big corporations or government organizations that have grown large in a short period of time. The network is constructed with different pieces using different topologies according to their needs. Then, as growth patterns dictate, the diverse networks are joined together into one big network layout.

The third method for classifying networks is by the standard that they use to transmit data. This is sometimes called the network architecture or *network protocol*. The three most common standards associated with PC networks include *Ethernet*, *Token Ring*, and *ArcNet*.

Ethernet: The most common standard. It uses either a bus or a star topology and either twisted-pair or RG-8 or RG-58 coax cabling to connect networked workstations. It can transmit 10 to 100 megabits per second (Mbps) and uses a CSMA/CD (carrier sense multiple access/collision detection) process for controlling data transmission. When a computer needs to send data, it checks the network for any traffic (carrier sense). If there is no traffic, it starts sending its data. All computers have access at all times to the network (multiple access). Two or more stations may check the network and start sending data at the same time, so the computer checks again to see whether the data have collided with other packets (collision detection). If a collision has occurred, the workstations wait a random time period and start the process all over again.

Token Ring: The standard used by IBM. It uses a ring topology and a token-passing process to send data. A special packet known as the *token* is passed continuously from workstation to workstation. Each computer is polled—if it has data to transmit, it is given a token it can use to start sending its data. At times, the token is lost. After a period of time, a new token will be generated. Data are transmitted only when a computer has a token. Token Ring networks transmit data at 4 to 16 Mbps over twisted pair or fiber optics.

ArcNet: Works with a physical bus or star topology that appears as a logical ring topology. It uses a token to pass between computers and has a data-transmit rate of between 2.5 and 10 Mbps over twisted pair, RG-62 coax, or fiber optics.

Network interface cards (NICs) must be designed for the topology (bus, ring, or star), standard (Ethernet, Token Ring, or ArcNet), and cable type (RG-8, RG-58, RG-62, twisted-pair, or fiber optics) of the network in which they will be installed.

A fourth method of classifying networks is by the type of *communication protocol* they use. A *protocol* is a set of rules that must be followed for everything to work right. The major protocols involved with setting up Windows-based networks include:

TCP/IP (Transmission Control Protocol/Internet Protocol): This protocol is a Unix-based communication standard used extensively on the Internet. Most networks support this feature today since it is the major communication protocol used throughout the Internet.

NetBIOS: This protocol is the standard used on IBM's networks.

NetBEUI: This protocol is the communications standard adopted by Microsoft for their networks. It is found in Windows 3.*x* and Windows 95.

IPX/SPX: This protocol is the proprietary network communication standard used by Novell.

Network Capabilities

Network capabilities include sharing networked resources such as disk drives, printers, and files. The capabilities of DOS and Windows are as follows:

- DOS by itself has no inherent ability to provide network services. Additional network software such as LANtastic by Artisoft and NetWare by Novell must be used to provide network capabilities.

- Both Windows 3.11 (Windows for Workgroups) and Windows 95 have built-in network capabilities. They can be set up in a peer-to-peer configuration using a bus topology and an Ethernet standard.

Some of the network services provided by Windows include:

Sharing of disk drives: Disk drives on each workstation can be shared between users of a peer-to-peer network. The owner of the disk drive must set up their system to allow the sharing of the drive or a directory on it, and the outside user must connect their workstation to the drive or directory opened to them. To the outside user, the connected drive appears as a local drive except that the icon for the drive uses a shared-drive symbol. The workstation with the shared drive or directory must have its computer turned on before the resource is available to the network, but the user does not have to be logged in. (On client/server systems, the shared drives are on the file server.)

Sharing of printers: On peer-to-peer networks, local printers can be shared with the network. The owner of the workstation that has the printer must set up their system for printer sharing. The outside users must set up their computers to connect to the shared printer. The workstation that has the shared printer must be turned on, but the user does not have to be logged on for the print services to work. (On client/server systems, the printers can be attached to a local workstation, to dedicated print servers, and as a node on the network cabling.)

Sharing of file services: Peer-to-peer users can set their systems up to share particular files with other users on the network. The drive must be indicated as a shared drive, but only the file or files in the directory that need to be shared are marked as shareable network files. When the outside user connects to the directory, the only files that are seen in the directory listing are the ones marked as shareable. These are the only files to which an outside user can gain access.

Workgroup services: Peer-to-peer networks also can declare workgroups and allow users to easily gain access to all the network resources they need for a particular team, project, or department. The owner of each workstation in the workgroup must make the necessary resources available to the network and connect to the resources they need on the other workstations. Then, they must identify the workgroup by giving it a name and possibly a password. When users log into the workgroup, all the resources are instantly made available to them as long as all the workstations in the group are turned on. All sorts of things can be done with a workgroup setup. You can share files and hardware, and you can set up a group schedule (with appointments, deadlines, etc.) to coordinate the efforts of the group.

Online chat: This service is for exchanging interactive messages between users on the network. If a person is not at their workstation, you cannot communicate with them.

In-house e-mail: E-mail is the ability to send a message to another user and leave it with the network if the person is not at their workstation. This is like sending a postcard to the person. When they receive the mail, they can respond to it.

Necessary Procedures

You should be familiar with the following procedures to pass the exam and perform your job duties:

- Setting up shared file services
- Setting up shared printers

Setting Up Shared Directories and File Services

To connect to a shared directory on a remote computer, you need to assign an unused local drive letter to it. The procedure for setting up a shared directory service in Windows 3.11 is as follows:

1. Make sure the remote computer has the directory set up as a shared resource by opening the File Manager on the remote computer, selecting the directory that you want to share, and then clicking the Share button on the toolbar.

2. Launch the File Manager to open the File Manager window.

3. Click the Connect Network Drive button on the toolbar to display the Connect Network Drive dialog box.

4. Specify the local drive letter you want to assign to the drive and type in the path to the shared directory using the remote computer's assigned name and the directory path.

5. To disconnect a network drive, click the Disconnect Drive button on the toolbar of the File Manager to display the list of network drives to which you are connected. Select the drive letter(s) you wish to disconnect from and click OK.

Setting up a shared disk drive is an easy way to overcome the problems associated with not having enough storage. The procedure for setting up shared file services in Windows 95 is as follows:

1. Open the Control Panel and double-click the Network icon to display the Network dialog box.

2. Click the File and Print Sharing button to display the File and Print Sharing dialog box (shown below).

3. Click the option you want to activate. In the case of sharing files, click the top checkbox labeled "I Want to Be Able to Give Others Access to My Files." Then, click OK to close the dialog box. Be ready to supply the Windows 95 CD-ROM if it is required.

4. Restart your computer by selecting Yes when asked whether you wish to do so.

5. You need to set up the drive you wish to share by opening My Computer, highlighting the drive, and then clicking the Sharing tab in the dialog box. Add the name, comment, access type (Read Only, Full, or Depends on Password), and optional password for the drive.

Setting Up a Shared Printer

The procedure for setting up a shared printer in Windows 3.11 is as follows:

1. Open the Print Manager window and select the printer you wish to share.

2. Click the Share Printer As button on the toolbar to display the Share Printer dialog box with the selected printer displayed in the Printer field.

3. Type in a name for the printer in the Share As field and a description for the printer in the Comments field. Enter a password only if you need to control printing.

4. To have the system set the printer as a network printer during boot up, click the Re-Share at Startup checkbox.

5. Click OK to activate the printer setup. Workstations will now be able to see the printer listed as a resource on the network.

The procedure for setting up a shared printer in Windows 95 is as follows:

1. Double-click the My Computer and Printers icons.

2. Right-click the printer you wish to share to display the printer's Properties page.

3. Click the Sharing tab and give the printer a network name and password if needed.

4. Click OK to close the Properties dialog box. The printer will be shareable at this time.

Exam Essentials

The A+ exam will test your knowledge of the types of networks and their characteristics, and your ability to set up services on a peer-to-peer network.

Know the different types of network classifications and their characteristics.   One way to classify networks is as client/server or peer to peer. Another way is by the type of their topology: bus, ring, star, or hybrid. Yet another way is by the standard or architecture they use to transmit data: Ethernet, Token Ring, or ArcNet.

Be familiar with the network capabilities provided by DOS and Windows.   There are no inherent network capabilities within DOS. Windows provides a built-in peer-to-peer network over which you can share files and printers.

Key Terms and Concepts

Chat: The network service that allows users to interact one on one much like using a typewriter over a telephone.

Client/server network: A network with a dedicated file server that provides services for workstations (clients) that request them.

E-mail: Electronic mail is the feature of a network that allows you to send letters, memos, and a variety of media (including sound and video) to other users on the network.

Local area network (LAN):   Two or more computers connected together within a department, business firm, or college campus. The area is usually restricted to a relatively small physical space.

Network architecture: The basic design of how the computer will connect to the network and send its data. It is a communications standard.

Network interface card (NIC):   The physical device that connects the network cabling to the computer. It is also called an interface card, network board, and other variations on the theme.

Network standard: See *Network architecture*.

Peer-to-peer network: A network in which there is no dedicated server. Each workstation provides services to other workstations and in turn receives services from the other workstations.

Topology: The physical layout of the devices on the network. A *star network* resembles a star with each workstation directly connected to a central file server or hub. A *bus network* has all the workstations connected to a single cable that is terminated on each end. A *ring network* connects all workstations with a cable that has both ends electrically connected to each other.

Sample Questions

1. Which topology or topologies is/are associated with Ethernet?

   A. Bus

   B. Ring

   C. Star

   D. ArcNet

   Answer: A, C. Ethernet can be used in both star and bus networks.

2. What are the network capabilities of DOS?

   A. File sharing

   B. Printer sharing

   C. Drive sharing

   D. None

   Answer: D. DOS, by itself, does not have any network capabilities.

Identify concepts and capabilities relating to the Internet and basic procedures for setting up a system for Internet access.

This objective concentrates on the concepts and capabilities of the Internet. You should focus on learning the different protocols, capabilities, and concepts associated with using the Internet as well as knowing how to set up a computer system for Internet access.

Critical Information

The Internet is becoming an essential tool in the modern office. All businesses both great and small are getting connected to the Internet for marketing, research, and/or communications purposes. The growth of the Internet and the businesses that are attached to it is increasing at an exponential rate, which guarantees that you will have to know how to set up a computer to access the Internet.

Being able to work with computers connected to the Internet will increase your value as a service technician. You will be expected to be familiar with the terms and concepts associated with the Internet, and have the abilities to troubleshoot and resolve Internet connection problems.

Before you can use the Internet, you must be connected to a LAN that has access to the Internet, or have an account with an Internet service provider (ISP) and have your modem set up to the ISP's specifications. Your modem should have at least a 9,600bps data-transfer rate. The faster the modem, the happier you will be. One consideration for a modem is the local data-transfer rate of your telephone company. In some areas, you may be able to transmit and receive data at a maximum rate of only 36.6Kbps or less due to the limitations of the telephone lines.

Transmission Control Protocol/Internet Protocol (TCP/IP)

TCP/IP is a suite of protocols designed to give you reliable data transfer across the Internet. Without TCP/IP, the Internet could not function. TCP/IP is divided into two basic components:

TCP: The transmission control protocol defines and controls the software portions of the data transfers.

IP: The Internet protocol defines and controls the hardware aspects of data transfers.

For your computer to access the Internet, you must set it up so that it will use TCP/IP as its protocol. This is accomplished as follows:

1. Open the Control Panel and the Network dialog box.

2. Click the Configuration page to bring it to the foreground.

3. Browse the list of network components to insure that the following lines are included as components:

   ```
   Dial-Up Adapter
   TCP/IP => Dial-Up Adapter
   ```

4. If they are not included in the list, click the Add button and add them. Be prepared to supply the Windows 95 installation CD-ROM.

Electronic Mail (E-Mail)

E-mail is a feature of a LAN or Web browser that allows users to send and receive mail across the network or the Internet. Before an e-mail program can work, it has to be set up to match the specifications of the network or the ISP. This is usually done through an option called Preferences or Options on the browser's menu bar. The following information must be entered on the setup page:

- Basic information about yourself, including name, address, and phone number

WARNING   Be aware that this information is often grabbed by Web sites for demographic analysis. If you do not want your name and phone number to be collected, give an alias for your name and leave out the phone number.

- Information about your ISP, and their Web and DNS address

- Information about your computer

- Information about your preferences for mail filters, etc.

Most e-mail packages allow you to include attachments when you send your message. Attachments can be either documents or graphics. It is usually a good idea to compress the files before they are sent. This reduces the overall file size, which improves throughput and also protects your documents from being corrupted in the transfer.

Some packages even let you attach uniform resource locators (URLs) of sites you may want someone to visit (such as your own home page). The URL is embedded in your document as a *hot link* to the Internet location. To the receiver, an embedded URL appears as an HTML hot link—when activated (clicked), it will send them to the Web address specified in the URL.

Hypertext Markup Language (HTML)

HTML is a page-description language that is used extensively throughout the World Wide Web to create Web pages. It provides a means of producing Web documents by adding tags to ASCII text files. The tags provide print enhancements, such as boldfacing and underlining, and the use of graphics within the document.

Hypertext Transfer Protocol (HTTP)

HTTP is a protocol that sets the criteria for World Wide Web (WWW) services. Its purpose is to provide an easy-to-use and totally transparent graphical method for creating and accessing data on the Internet. It is the basis for the operations of the WWW. HTTP is activated through a daemon called HTTPD on a WWW server.

File Transfer Protocol (FTP)

FTP is the Internet protocol for transferring files between hosts. When you download a program, FTP runs in the background providing you with this capability. FTP gives you the ability to log onto another computer, perform limited directory maneuvers, and download or upload files. To use FTP to download a file:

1. Log into your Internet site and start FTP on your computer by either using a menu provided by your ISP or typing **ftp** at the command prompt.

2. When the FTP prompt appears, type **OPEN** *FTP_Address* to connect to the remote computer (*FTP_Address* is the address of the other computer).

3. At the login prompt from the other computer, type **ANONYMOUS** and enter your e-mail address for the password.

4. Once the login has been completed, you can use the CD and CDUP commands to negotiate the other computer's file system.

5. When you find a file you want to download, use the GET command. Since most FTP sites are UNIX-based systems, you need to enter all command lines in lowercase.

Domain Names (Web Sites)

Domain names are names given to an organizational unit responsible for naming hosts and networks. Some of the more common domain names are as follows:

EDU Educational organizations
COM Commercial organizations
NFP Not-for-profit organizations
GOV Government organizations
NET Network entities such as ISPs

The domain administration facilitates the assignment of names to organizations that wish to establish their Web presence by creating their own Web site.

A Web site is an Internet location that belongs to an organization or person and is where the organization or person creates their home page. Whenever you transfer to a URL or IP address on the World Wide Web, you will enter the Web site for the organization or individual who owns the site.

Internet Service Provider (ISP)

The *ISP* is the company that provides you with dial-up access to the Internet. They give you the necessary software and disk space to connect to and work within the Internet. They have the Web servers that interconnect with the Internet system. Some of the services they offer include:

- Dial-up connections
- E-mail
- News
- Individual home pages

ISPs can be classified into three basic groups: local, regional, and national. Local ISPs provide services to a small geographical area such as a town or county. Regional ISPs provide services on a larger basis such as a state or an entire region (e.g., the Midwest). National ISPs provide services throughout the country.

Dial-Up Access

Dial-up access is the basic means of connecting to the Internet through an ISP. You must have a modem or an ISDN device on your computer that is supported by the telephone company that services your phone and the ISP.

In Windows 95, you must have the Dial-Up Networking folder installed on your computer. This folder will contain the setup utility to add a new connection, and a connection icon for each ISP or modem with which you have connections. Figure 5.1 shows the Dial-Up Networking folder and the starting screen for the Make New Connection utility.

FIGURE 5.1: Dial-Up Networking

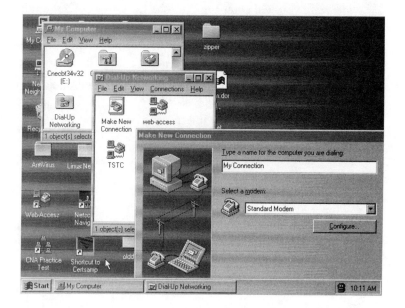

Installing an ISP connection requires the setup utility provided by the ISP. If you don't have one, you can create a connection manually. For manual installation, you need the primary and secondary DNS addresses, the phone number of the ISP server, the modem settings for their communications channel, the type of server they have, and the protocol they use. Create a new connection (see below), right-click the new connection, and fill in the fields with the appropriate information.

To create a new connection, you use the Make New Connection icon and configure the modem, list the user's name, enter the ISP's phone number that the modem will dial, define the location from which you will be dialing, and set the dialing properties.

To change the ISP information, right-click the Connection icon and select Properties from the pop-up menu. Set the type of dial-up server you will be connecting to, define the type of network protocol used by the server, and, in the case of TCP/IP, set the primary and secondary DNS addresses.

Exam Essentials

The A+ exam will test your knowledge of the Internet and how to connect to it.

Know the primary communications protocol used on the Internet.   The primary protocol used on the Internet is TCP/IP.

Be familiar with the more common terms associated with the Internet.   The terms and concepts you will most likely be tested on include e-mail, HTML, FTP, domain names, ISP, and dial-up access.

Know how to set up Windows 95 for an Internet connection.   To set up Windows 95 for Internet connection, you must use the Make New Connection icon in the Dial-Up Networking folder, and fill in the fields to set up your modem and configure your connection to the settings of your ISP.

Key Terms and Concepts

Bits per second (bps):   The measure of modem speed. The larger the bps value, the faster the modem.

Browser: An application that allows you to search through or surf the Internet.

Domain name service (DNS):   A distributed database used by TCP/IP to locate the proper host by converting the host's name to the host's IP address.

Hot link: A hypertext link within a document that allows you to transfer to another URL by double-clicking the hot link. The link is considered hot while it is still active.

Internet: A network of other larger networks. It is a global network that uses the TCP\IP protocol.

Internet service provider (ISP): A company that provides dial-up access to the Internet.

News filters: Software controls used to pass only the information categories designated by the receiver.

Protocol: A set of rules and specifications that determine how a communication channel will work.

World Wide Web (WWW): A global system of interconnected networks offering HTTP services for users who have compatible browsers.

Sample Questions

1. What is the protocol used in Windows 95 for peer-to-peer networking?

A. TCP/IP

B. NetBIOS

C. NetBEUI

D. IPX/SPX

Answer: C. Even though Windows will install both IPX/SPX and NetBEUI by default, NetBEUI is the only protocol needed by Windows 95 (unless you are running another network operating system).

2. What protocol is used on the World Wide Web?

    A. TCP/IP

    B. NetBIOS

    C. NetBEUI

    D. IPX/SPX

Answer: A. TCP/IP is used on the Internet.

Index

NOTE: Page numbers in *italics* refer to figures; page numbers in **bold** refer to significant discussions of the topic

W

warm boots, 60, 100
warm docking, 144
Web sites, **236–237**
wildcard characters, 39, 43
WIN386.EXE, 15
WIN386.SWP file, 84
WIN.COM, 15, 130–131
WINDELETE, 190
windows, 11
   expanding to full-screen, 36
   term defined, 39
Windows 3.11
   network capabilities, 227
   for peer-to-peer network, 223
   shared printer setup on, 230
Windows 3.*x*
   boot-up process, **130–131**
     common problems, **171–172**
   components of, 10–11, 23
   device drivers for, 109, **141**
   display elements, 24
   emergency boot disk, 135–136
   filenames in, **42**
   functions of, 7–8, 23
   illegal operations errors in, 189
   installing, **101–104, 114–116**
   installing and launching applications under,
     160–161, 163
   installing printer, **180–181**
   memory management by, 83–85
   minimum requirements for, 101–102,
     118–119
   navigating, **30**
   opening, 33
   printer setup under, **154**
   printing in, **152–153**, 177–178
   problem solving improprer running, 193
   setting file attributes, **45**
   system, configuration & user-interface files,
     18–20
   system files for, 14–15
   troubleshooting GPF, 187
   upgrading to Windows 95 from, **123–124**
   virtual memory in, 84–85
   versus Windows 95, **11–13**
Windows 95
   and 16-bit applications conflicts, **89–90**, 92
   boot-up process, **131–133**
     common problems, **172–173**
     multi-boot capability, 134
   components of, 11, 24
   data file access methods, 37

   device drivers for, 109, **124, 141–145**
   Device Manager, *203*, 203–204
   Dial-Up Networking, 237, *238*
   display elements, 24
   filenames in, **42–43**, 47
   functions of, 8–9
   GPF errors in, 188
   hardware requirements, 105
   illegal operations errors in, 189
   installing, **104–106, 116–117**
   installing and launching applications under,
     161–162, 163
   installing printer, **181–182**
   memory heaps in, 86
   memory management by, 85–87
   methods to access data files, 37
   navigating, **30**
     with Explorer, *35*, 35–36
     with My Computer, *36*, 36–37
     with Start menu, **34**, *35*
   network capabilities, 227
   for peer-to-peer network, 223
   Print Troubleshooter, *178*, 178–179
   printer setup under, **155–156**
   printing in, 153, **177–178**
   setting attributes in, 43–44, **45–46**
   shared printer setup on, 230–231
   Startup Disk, 136
   switches to load from command prompt, 135
   system and user-interface files, 20
   system files, 15
   upgrade to, **122–127**
   Windows 3.*x* versus, **11–13**
WINFILE.INI, 131
WIN.INI, 109, 131, 132
   in Windows 3.*x*, 19
   in Windows 95, 16, 110
wizard, 120, 127
word processor, for editing system files, 118
workgroup services, 228
World Wide Web (WWW), 240
worms, 208, 218

X

XCOPY command (DOS), 7
XT computer, 80

A+ TEST PREPARATION FROM THE EXPERTS

Sybex presents the most comprehensive study guides for CompTIA's 1998 A+ exams for PC technicians.

ISBN 0-7821-2344-9
800 pp. 7½" x 9" $49.99
Hardcover July 1998

ISBN 0-7821-2351-1
688 pp. 7½" x 9" $49.99
Hardcover July 1998

ISBN 0-7821-2380-5
1,488 pp. 7½" x 9" $84.98
Hardcover 2-volume box set
August 1998

ISBN 0-7821-2345-7
304 pp. 5⅞" x 8¼" $19.99
Softcover August 1998

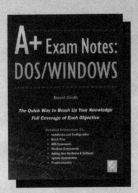

ISBN 0-7821-2346-5
304 pp. 5⅞" x 8¼" $19.99
Softcover August 1998

SYBEX
www.sybex.co

MCSE ELECTIVE STUDY GUIDES FROM NETWORK PRESS®

Sybex's Network Press expands the definitive study guide series for MCSE candidates.

ISBN: 0-7821-2224-8
688pp; 7¹/₂" x 9"; Hardcover
$49.99

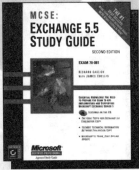

ISBN: 0-7821-2261-2
848pp; 7¹/₂" x 9"; Hardcover
$49.99

ISBN: 0-7821-2248-5
704pp; 7¹/₂" x 9"; Hardcover
$49.99

ISBN: 0-7821-2172-1
672pp; 7¹/₂" x 9"; Hardcover
$49.99

ISBN: 0-7821-2194-2
576pp; 7¹/₂" x 9"; Hardcover
$49.99

ISBN: 0-7821-1967-0
656pp; 7¹/₂" x 9"; Hardcover
$49.99

Microsoft Certified
Professional
Approved Study Guide

STUDY GUIDES FOR THE MICROSOFT CERTIFIED SYSTEMS ENGINEER EXAM